A YEAR IN THE LIFE OF CHRIST SERIES
2
The Power of Jesus
Group Study
STUDIES FOR SMALL GROUPS
Mark Moore
&
Jon Weece
C0-CEO-026

Copyright © 2002
College Press Publishing Co.
On the web at www.collegepress.com

All Scripture quotations, unless indicated, are taken from
THE HOLY BIBLE: NEW INTERNATIONAL VERSION®.
Copyright © 1973, 1978, 1984 by International Bible Society.
Used by permission of Zondervan Publishing House.
All rights reserved.

Cover design by Mark A. Cole

International Standard Book Number 0-89900-848-8

TABLE OF CONTENTS

Introduction: The Finger of God ◇◇◇◇◇◇◇◇◇◇◇◇◇◇◇◇◇◇◇◇ 5

1 To Heal Outcasts and Command Inanimate Forces (Matthew 8:1-17) ◇◇◇◇◇◇◇◇◇◇ 7

2 Through the Roof (Luke 5:17-26) ◇◇◇◇◇◇◇◇◇◇◇◇◇◇◇◇◇◇◇◇ 14

3 Satan's Card House (Matthew 12:22-37) ◇◇◇◇◇◇◇◇◇◇◇◇◇◇◇◇ 21

4 Master of Raging Storms and Raving Demoniacs (Mark 4:35–5:20) ◇◇◇◇◇◇◇◇◇◇◇◇◇ 27

5 Lord over Blood and Death (Mark 5:21-43) ◇◇◇◇◇◇◇◇◇◇ 34

6 Hail to the Chief (Matthew 10:1-42) ◇◇◇◇◇◇◇◇◇◇◇◇◇◇◇◇◇◇ 40

7 Lord of All Creation (Matthew 14:13-36) ◇◇◇◇◇◇◇◇◇◇◇◇◇◇ 46

8 Unwashed Hands and a New View of Humanity (Matthew 15:1-20) ◇◇◇◇◇◇◇◇◇◇◇◇ 53

9 Transfiguration:
God in the Flesh (Matthew 17:1-13) ◇◇◇◇◇◇◇◇◇◇◇◇◇◇◇◇◇◇◇◇◇◇◇◇ 59

10 The Mirror of the Blind Man (John 9:1-41) ◇◇◇◇◇◇◇◇ 65

11 The Power of Jesus over Death (John 11:1-44) ◇◇◇◇◇◇◇◇ 72

12 Jesus' Last Two "Converts" (Luke 18:35–19:10) ◇◇◇◇◇◇◇◇◇◇ 78

13 Cleansing the Temple (Mark 11:15-18) ◇◇◇◇◇◇◇◇◇◇◇◇◇◇◇◇◇◇ 85

THE FINGER OF GOD

Magicians and power-lifters sure are fun to watch. They can just do cool stuff, like cutting people in half and ripping phone books. We watch the magician and ask, "How did he do that?" We watch the strong man and say, "There's just no way!" They inflame our curiosity through their uncanny abilities. Jesus does too; only there is a qualitative difference.

Remember when the magicians of Egypt tried to compete with Moses? After several inept imitations they finally gave up. They waved the white flag when they declared, "We can't do that. He performs his miracles by the very ***finger of God***!" (Exod. 8:19). Flash forward to Jesus' ministry (Luke 11:20). When accused by the Pharisees of casting out demons by the power of Beelzebub he hearkened back to this incident saying, "I've overcome the strongman, and done this by the ***finger of God***." Jesus is not just another exorcist, manipulating the spiritual forces of this world. He is the very presence of God in this world.

He is not like a magician who uses smoke and mirrors or sleight of hand. He is the Logos who creates out of nothing through the sheer power of his will. He's no mere steroid-induced athlete who can perform Herculean acts of strength. He is Yahweh incarnate who gives orders to the raging elements and stills both wind and wave. He's not some guru or monk well-connected to the cosmos. He is the Son of God who speaks with the Divine on a first-name basis. He's neither priest nor pope nor T.V. evangelist that conjures up authority by counsel or creed. His words are Life and Truth which inherently deserve to be capitalized.

So many "nice" things are said about him. He's equated with a good teacher, a kind healer, a compassionate social worker, a charismatic philosopher, etc., etc. All are true, but none are sufficient. To suggest that Jesus is anything less than Yahweh incarnate is to "damn him with faint praise."

In this series of lessons we will take a look at the power of Jesus. We will wonder at his miracles. We will cower at the raw power of his words. We will bow before his mighty hand that feeds 5,000 and cleanses a temple. We will come before him as the only one who can save us, yet tread lightly out of respect. One such as Jesus ought not to be trifled with. We shall, I pray, both gasp at his striking power, and sigh in relief that he exercises it graciously on our behalf.

If you are merely investigating Jesus, we invite you to join our study. Come in openly; you are welcome. Come, however, with joyful reverence. Be prepared to be undone by what you find in this peasant Galilean. Be prepared to be recreated in his image.

If you are a seasoned saint, we welcome you too. This investigation never grows old; Christ is ever the same and always new. The same Jesus you've loved and served will meet you again in fresh and startling ways. The power of Jesus will overwhelm you like never before just as it always has.

Most people are brought to faith in Christ not by argument for it but by exposure to it.

—*Samuel M. Shoemaker*

1 1

TO HEAL OUTCASTS AND COMMAND INANIMATE FORCES

1 1

Text: Matthew 8:1-17 **Memory:** Matthew 8:10-12

Leap of Faith In the October 1993 issue of *Life* magazine, a photo shot by Scott Threlkeld shows three teenage boys who have jumped from a thirty-foot-high cypress branch toward a dark Louisiana pond. Threlkeld evidently climbed the tree and shot from above the shirtless, soaring Huck Finns, for in the picture we look down on the boys and the pond. There is something inspiring in the picture.

The lanky boy on the right shows the least confidence, jumping feet first, knees bent and legs spread, arms flapping like a bird prepared to make a crash landing. The middle boy dives head first, arms spread stiffly straight and perpendicular, like the wings of a small aircraft. His head is slightly ducked and to the right. He is no doubt in a hurry to reach the water. The third boy also dives head first, but he isn't in a hurry. He is floating. His head is up. His body is in a relaxed arch, both knees slightly bent, legs slightly apart. His arms are nonchalantly straight, hanging from his shoulders in an upside-down V. Poised and self-assured, he knows exactly where he is.

No matter their sense or style, each of these three boys did a challenging thing: He took a scary leap. Granted, high dives into country backwaters aren't always wise, but sometimes to follow God we must take a similar leap of faith. When we do, like the three people we are preparing to meet in the next few pages, we will find that the kingdom of God is sometimes in the pond and beyond.

Overview of the Text

We're looking here at three stories: a leper, a centurion, and a woman. They are all so different, yet they belong together since none of them belong. They are outsiders, all of them. It's not surprising to find them lumped together here in Matthew's book. He knows what it's like to be rejected. He also knows what it's like to follow Jesus and to be used by God. He tells their story not because the raw details are so interesting. There is a subtext here, a theme that is essential for the church to grasp.

Pondering the Power of Jesus

- In what ways do you identify with the leper, the centurion, and the woman in this chapter? Have you ever felt like an outsider?
- What obstacles are in the way of your developing a faith similar to that of the centurion who approached Jesus? Is it doubt? A painful past? An unhealthy habit?
- How does your church view outsiders? How can you get on the solution side of that discussion?

Meaning of the Text

Matthew 8–9 hang together as a distinct literary unit tucked between two famous sermons. At first, it looks like a random collection of healings and "stuff." Upon closer examination, however, there is a definite pattern:

Sermon on the Mount, 5–7	
3 outsiders healed (8:1-17)	Discussion of **discipleship** (8:18-22)
3 stories about Jesus' power over the forces of nature, demons, and sickness/sin (8:23–9:8)	A call of a **disciple** (9:9-17)
Two paired healings: 2 women (9:18-26) & 2 blind men and a demoniac (9:27-34)	A charge to his **disciples** (9:35-38)
Sermon on Sending the Twelve, 10.	

Matthew alternates between descriptions of healings and discussion of discipleship. He intends to suggest that they go hand in glove. None of these healings are recounted simply to demonstrate Jesus' power. They are "enacted parables" which describe Jesus' program. They are glimpses into the kind of kingdom he wants to establish. In this lesson we will look at the first of the three miracles in an attempt to understand what Jesus intends the church to be.

Look at them as they stand side by side in Matthew 8—a leper, a centurion, and a woman. Each has his/her own story, but all fall into the same category: Outsider.

The leper was an outsider because his disease rendered him unclean. The word "leper" literally means, "to peal." That's a nasty name for a skin condition any way you slice it. This curse is described in Leviticus 13. It sounds like some kind of fungus that could migrate to leather, pottery, and even walls of a home. It caused reddish-white sores that festered. A leper was a human scab that was ostracized from the community. He was required to cry out "unclean" when anyone approached. The rabbis, who were most persnickety about cleanness, were the meanest to these poor pariahs. One Pharisee even boasted that he pelted lepers with rocks to keep them at bay. What makes matters worse is that the disease had a stigma of sin attached to it. In other words, those with leprosy were assumed to have been smitten by God for some secret offense.

Under these circumstances, it is amazing that the leper approached Jesus to ask for help. No other rabbi demonstrated either the interest or ability to heal leprosy. There was apparently something in Jesus that solicited such extraordinary faith. Against all odds, this poor fellow asks Jesus for help. Against the rules, Jesus touches him. The crowd gasps. The leper is clean. All is well.

The centurion was an outsider because he was a Gentile. Worse than that, he was a "lieutenant" in the enemy's occupational forces. One would think he would be hated. In actuality, he was loved by the Jewish people. Why? Because he helped them build their synagogue. Why would he do that? Well, the Middle East was a culture of patron/client relationships. The patrons offered their clients protection, resources, and security. The clients offered their patron honor, fidelity, and service. This centurion wisely perceived that the Jewish community in which he served would better serve him if they were all on the same side. Thus, he put his money where they put their hearts—the synagogue. He built well; the black basalt foundation of this building can still be seen to this day.

The centurion was a beloved "god-fearer." But he had a problem. One of his trusted servants, kind of adopted into his family, was paralyzed in bed with some crippling illness. The elders come to Jesus on behalf of this military officer (cf. Luke 7:1-10). He is willing to help. In fact, he is willing to go into the guy's house to raise the young man. Obviously, that is going to raise a few eyebrows and perhaps cause Jesus a bit of trouble. So the centurion stops him short. "I'm a military man," he says. "I give commands and my men jump. I receive commands and I obey. I know how this works. You don't need to enter my home, just give the command and the sickness will be gone."

Don't misunderstand what the officer is saying. He is not suggesting that Jesus can command inanimate forces. No, the ancients believed sickness was caused by certain spiritual entities (gods or demons). Thus, the centurion is saying to Jesus, "Just as I command human beings, you are a ruler of the unseen spiritual powers." Wow. This guy gets it! In fact, Jesus was amazed, which is amazing in and of itself. After all, how are you going to amaze Jesus: With your incredible musical ability? With your prowess in preaching? With your good looks or great intelligence? No, the only thing that amazes Jesus is our faith in him (or lack thereof, cf. Mark 6:5).

Peter's mother-in-law was an outsider simply because she was a woman. Now, that's not a nice thing to say, but it was true. Women were second-class citizens. Here we have an old woman who is sick. Peter goes to bat for her and asks Jesus to see what he can do. In no time the woman is up and around. The first thing she does is serve them. It was the Sabbath but the rumor mill was still running with a full head of steam. News got out about the old lady, and as soon as the sun set, here they came with the sick in tow. There were bandages, crutches, cots, and the stench of festering sores. They lined the streets in search of relief. This time they'll not be disappointed. Jesus meanders through the streets, carefully ministering renewal to each one. He moves through a crowd of groaning patients, throbbing with pain. In his wake he leaves the kingdom of God with its trappings of laughter, dancing, and pulsating joy.

So what is Matthew trying to tell us? Considering the fact that he was one of these outsiders at one time, his message is crucial. First, this is an invitation to come to Jesus. To all the sundry hoi polloi Matthew says, "Come! You too are welcome . . . you *especially* are welcome." For those who are sick or disfigured, the leper says, "Come." To the ethnic minority or the politically disenfranchised, the centurion says, "Come." To the powerless and voiceless, this mother-in-law says, "Come." You may not feel like much. That's okay, you fit here.

Second, not only are the outsiders welcome in the kingdom, they receive preference. They are the ones who most impressed Jesus. The leper had the chutzpah to charge up to the master and plead for help. The centurion had the faith Jesus tried in vain to find in Israel. Peter's mother-in-law rose from the bed to serve at the table. These three are model disciples. Now, let's dispel this silly notion that the poor receive preference because the rich have already had their chance. This is not an "evening of the score" in God's divine economy. The rich, the beautiful, the powerful are just as welcomed to the kingdom. The reason the poor receive preference is because they are more acutely aware of their need. It is difficult to convince the comfortable that Christ is essential. They have so many options, so many resources to fall back on. But a leper, a centurion, and an old woman have nothing else, no other resources, no other options. So they lay prostrate before the Lord and beseech his help. Anyone who does that will quickly find the resources of God at their best.

Finally, each of these three foreshadows the cross. The leper's hopeless condition and aura of sin is eradicated by the touch of the master. The centurion's story will be repeated in Acts 10 through another centurion who was the first actual Gentile convert to Christ. He foreshadows the crumbling walls of ethnocentrism and the freedom for all to enter the kingdom. Peter's mother-in-law sparked a healing revival that must have been a foretaste of heaven. After Jesus healed the last person that night, he surely turned to survey the city. Through the glimmering light of the moon, all he could see were bandages, crutches, and cots littering the empty streets. There were no more tears or pain for Satan's work had been reversed. If the kingdom of God is victorious even among the outcasts, where can it not go? Your home?

Participating in the Power of Jesus

Take the time to visit a children's hospital, a cancer wing, or a hospice with people suffering from AIDS. Establish relationships with some patients. Pray for them, encourage them, visit them, and share the comfort and peace of Jesus with them and their families.

2

THROUGH THE ROOF

We teach what we know; we reproduce what we are.
—Robert Schmidgall

Text: Luke 5:17-26 **Memory:** Luke 5:22-24

Live between Steps

A university professor tells of being invited to speak at a military base one December and meeting there an unforgettable soldier named Ralph. Ralph had been sent to meet him at the airport. After they had introduced themselves, they headed toward the baggage claim.

As they walked down the concourse, Ralph kept disappearing. Once to help an older woman whose suitcase had fallen open. Once to lift two toddlers up to where they could see Santa Claus, and again to give directions to someone who was lost. Each time he came back with a smile on his face.

"Where did you learn that?" the professor asked.

"What?" Ralph said.

"Where did you learn to live like that?"

"Oh," Ralph said, "during the war, I guess." He then told

the professor about his tour of duty in Vietnam, how it was his job to clear mine fields, and how he watched his friends blow up before his very eyes, one after another.

"I learned to live between steps," he said. "I never knew whether the next one would be my last, so I learned to get everything I could out of the moment between when I picked up my foot and when I put it down again. Every step I took was a whole new world, and I guess I've been that way ever since."

Jesus is preparing not only to teach a paralytic to walk again, but by forgiving his sins he will free him to enjoy every step, and every moment in between.

Overview of the Text

The Hatfields and the McCoys, Palestinians and Israelis, Irish Catholics and Protestants, KKK & Malcolm X—these are explosive combinations. Read carefully Luke 5:17 and you'll hear of another: The Pharisees from Jerusalem and Jesus' healing power. They mix kind of like gasoline and a sparkler. Right from the get-go you know something is about to blow. Jesus seems especially adept at inflaming such volatile situations. Before all is said and done he'll be labeled a blasphemer. Why? Because he offered a lame man forgiveness of sins—a prerogative that belongs exclusively to God. The fireworks are about to begin.

Pondering the Power of Jesus

- What do you think was going through the lame man's mind when he was carried by his friends? When he interrupted the sermon? When the Pharisees got upset? When he walked out of there?
- Can you remember (and share) a moment when you truly felt forgiven by Jesus? What was it like?
- Does Jesus really have the prerogative to forgive sins? What about yours? What sins have you not given over to him—what regrets do you still keep as personal property?

Meaning of the Text

Up to now Jesus' ministry has been relatively serene. Oh sure, there was that little foray in the wilderness with Satan, but in terms of human opposition, it's been quite calm. He simply has not yet gained the kind of popularity that attracts the attention of the religious elite or national politicians. All that is about to change. His cleansing of the temple in Jerusalem and his healings in Galilee are opening a few eyes as the gossip mills grind out fabulous stories. A delegation of Pharisees from all over the area assemble to hear what the upstart has to say. At this point they are not unfriendly toward him, just curious. Even his cleansing of the temple would not affect the Pharisees as much as the Sadducees. This Jesus character just might be all right. That's what they're here to decide.

After an itinerant preaching tour and healing campaign, Jesus returns to Capernaum (Mark 2:1). This little city on the north shore of the lake of Galilee had become his headquarters. Apparently some well-to-do family had allowed Jesus to set up shop in their home. It had to have been a fairly large house since it hosted Jesus' sermon that day. Normally these larger homes were built around a central square. They were often two, sometimes three stories with the doors to each room opening into the courtyard in the middle. They also tended to build awnings around the perimeter of the courtyard so people could gather, work, and talk outside their rooms but still be shaded from the sun and rain. Our best guess is that a crowd had crammed into the courtyard to hear Jesus preach. He likely stood just outside this room underneath the awning. That's when things got interesting.

While Jesus preaches, the crowds swarm. There's a lot of sickness in the third-world conditions of Palestine. Medical help is scarce, and Jesus is always on the move. Therefore, when he's in town, you better get at him while the gettin' is good. Crowds shove their way into this courtyard. The Pharisees watch with amazement and, if the truth be told, a good bit of envy. Jesus begins to preach. Outside the gate a few latecomers show up. You can't really blame them for being tardy; after all, they had to carry their paralytic friend. But now they can't squeeze in. They're desperate to have their buddy healed and their throbbing triceps remind them why.

Somehow they climb up on the roof, possibly through the house next door with the help of a long plank. Nonetheless, they manhandle a nervous paralytic up a couple of flights of stairs and then down onto the awning that surprisingly held the weight of five grown men. Based on the direction of the crowd, they estimate where Jesus would be standing. There they start to dig. Since the awning was built from sticks and thatch, they are able to disassemble an entire section and lower their friend through the opening. Meanwhile, Jesus is trying to preach through this significant distraction. With the giggles and pointing and falling debris it is undoubtedly difficult to keep his train of thought. Suddenly a large beam of light floods through the awning. Then comes a rectangular eclipse, the shape of a pallet. Once the lame man is about waist level Jesus can see his impish grin. The four vandals look on with interest from above.

Now there were a number of things Jesus could have said. But no one would have predicted what actually came out of his mouth: "Your sins are forgiven." One wonders how much sin a paralytic could actually get himself into! Nevertheless, the Jewish idea of sickness was most often connected with sin. In other words, if this guy is afflicted so severely, either he or his parents had to have done something really, really bad. Obviously, Jesus is not buying into that false notion here anymore than he did with the blind man in Jerusalem (cf. John 9:1-2). However, we need to be aware that in the mind of Jesus' audience, sin and sickness were, in fact, connected. This sentence, "Your sins are forgiven," would be understood as a promise to release the man from his paralysis. However, Jesus won't treat him as a physician or magician would. He would deal with it in ways that only God could.

When Jewish psychiatrist Victor Frankl was arrested by the Nazis in World War II, he was stripped of everything—property, family, possessions, and dignity. He had spent years researching and writing a book on the importance of finding meaning in life. When he arrived in Auschwitz, the infamous death camp, even his manuscript, which he had hidden in the lining of his coat, was taken away. He surrendered his clothes and inherited the worn out rags of an inmate who had already been sent to the gas chamber. When Frankl searched the pockets of his newly acquired clothing, he found a single page torn out of a Hebrew prayer book that contained the main Jewish prayer, the Shema Yisrael. He didn't see the find as a coincidence, rather he recognized the challenge to live out his thoughts, instead of merely putting them on paper. He later completed his book, *Man's Search for Meaning* and wrote, "There is nothing in the world that would so effectively help one survive even the worst conditions, as the knowledge that there is a meaning in one's life . . . He who has a *why* to live for can bear almost any *how*."

Jesus' comment certainly doesn't slip by the watching Pharisees. They thought to themselves, "Why does this fellow talk like that? That's blasphemy! Only God can forgive sins." They ask *why* because they didn't have a *why* to live for! They didn't have a relationship with God, they had a relationship with his law, which sadly had left them spiritually paralyzed. And because they didn't have a *why* to live for, they questioned *how* Jesus was able to claim such authority. A couple of things should be clarified here. First, blasphemy is any kind of an insult. Although Jesus hasn't cursed God or called him a bad name, he has claimed prerogatives that belong only to the divine. Thus, Jesus was "bringing Yahweh down to his level" in the minds of the Pharisees. That's what irritated them. They apparently underestimated the promise of "Immanuel" ("God with us") from Isaiah 7:14. Second, while humans are obligated to forgive one another of personal trespasses, only God can remit the legal/spiritual liability of sin. In other words, if you beat me up, I'm able to forgive you so that we can still be friends. But you are still going to be liable to the law when the officer drags you from my pummeled carcass. I can say, "I forgive him" all I want. That's not going to get the cuffs off. Jesus is not here offering personal forgiveness for an offense suffered. He is absolving a man's transgression against God! Is it any small wonder the Pharisees protested?

Jesus knows their thoughts. (I doubt it took any special omniscience to figure out why their faces were all screwed up and they were contorting in their seats!) He laid out a bit of logic: "Which is easier to say, 'Your sins are forgiven,' or 'Get up and walk'?" This passage used to puzzle me. In fact, in junior high I actually counted the number of syllables—they are virtually the same. The point is, both are easy to say but impossible *to do* without the power of God. It is impossible to see with the naked eye the forgiveness of sins. Paralysis, on the other hand, is easy to test empirically. Thus, if Jesus can do the one, which is seen, we must also believe that he has done the other, which is not seen.

With that the Master turns to the man lying before him and orders him to pick up his pallet and walk. He does—straight through the crowd that had earlier kept him out. Apparently they were now able to find a bit of room they had denied was there before. With that, the argument is obviously over, but the conflict had only just begun. This question of Jesus' authority to forgive sins was one of the key battlegrounds of his ministry. Wrapped up in this question was the whole issue of Jesus' authority as well as his mission to establish God's kingdom through redemption. We see here shades of the cross as well as a reflection of our own pilgrimage. We too come to Jesus with problems we want fixed. To our surprise, dismay, and delight, he roots out the core problem—our sin. And all the rest disappears as we stand on our feet once again. This image of a lame man walking so powerfully pictures the life of the disciple that Luke records it two other times, once by the hand of Peter (Acts 3:6-9) and once by Paul (Acts 14:8-10). Both of these healings in Acts are followed by significant sermons explaining the person of Jesus and the hope we have in him. Thus, we have a strategic trilogy. Taken together, they don't tell of the story of dramatic power to heal, but of the person of Jesus who can eradicate our sins.

Now there is one more critical issue to consider before we close: Are you allowing Jesus to do with you what he did with the lame man? We lay before him our family or job, our health or finances. We ask him to "fix us." He has something deeper in mind. We go to church for a weekly dose. He demands daily discipleship. Listen, friend, Jesus doesn't want to give you cosmetic surgery, he is prescribing a heart transplant. If you could only allow him to forgive your sins, you would see he is capable of such deep spiritual surgery. If you come to him flat on your back, you will surely hear him say, "Rise and walk."

Participating in the Power of Jesus

There are four types of people in this narrative:

The *helpers* . . . carried their friend to Jesus.
The *hinderers* . . . prevented the paralytic from getting close to Jesus.
The *healed* . . . a paralytic man set free.

Jesus takes on the role of the *healer* and does it well. Jesus is calling you to be a "healed helper" not a "healed hinderer." One of the ways you can help others experience what you've experienced is by establishing a prayer ministry in your church. Create a prayer list of people in your church or community who need the healing touch of Jesus. Pray for local and global leaders to experience the relationship with Jesus that you have. Meet with your minister and ask him/her to teach on the subject. Prayer is foundational to spiritual and physical healing. By establishing a prayer ministry in your church, you will see Jesus work as he did on the man lowered through the roof.

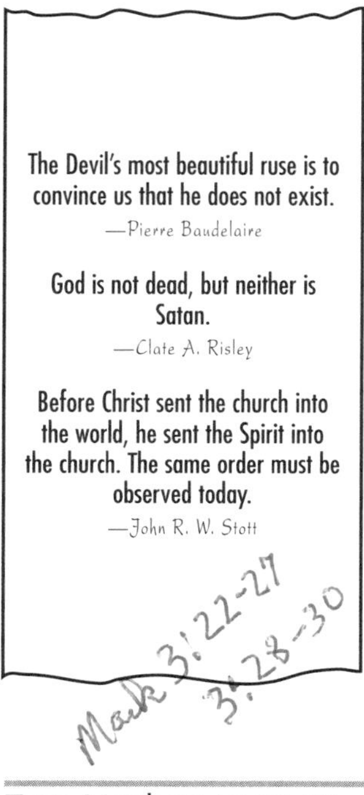

The Devil's most beautiful ruse is to convince us that he does not exist.

—Pierre Baudelaire

God is not dead, but neither is Satan.

—Clate A. Risley

Before Christ sent the church into the world, he sent the Spirit into the church. The same order must be observed today.

—John R. W. Stott

3

SATAN'S CARD HOUSE

Text: Matthew 12:22-37 **Memory:** Matthew 12:30

Evil Personified

Al Capone is America's best known gangster and the single greatest symbol of the collapse of law and order in the United States during the 1920s Prohibition era. His city of operation was Chicago and it became known as a "lawless" city.

Capone was born on January 17, 1899, in Brooklyn, New York. He grew up in a rough neighborhood and was a member of two gangs. He quit school in the sixth grade and soon landed a job as a bouncer in a local bar owned by a notorious mobster. It was in that bar that Capone received a nickname, a mark that would last. He was cut on the face by a patron, and from that day forward was known as "Scarface."

He was smart and worked his way into a position of leadership and eventually control. His downfall began with an ill-planned shooting. Although Al Capone didn't understand it at the time, the Valentine's Day Massacre catalyzed the government forces against him and the underworld operations he ran. Capone was a bootlegger, a thief, a murderer, and a liar. He took pride in each of those labels and made a name for himself as one of the worst criminals in American History. J. Edgar Hoover, who was the director of the FBI in Capone's day, created the FBI's list of the "10 Most Wanted" criminals. Capone's name was at the top of that list.

The case against Capone was spearheaded by Hoover and a little-known IRS agent named Eliot Ness. On June 5, 1931, a grand jury met and returned an indictment against Capone with twenty-two counts of tax evasion. It seems petty, a tax evasion charge, but it was the only way to bring Capone and his gang to justice. A man who made a living by scaring people into submission, a man people called untouchable, eventually met his match.

Read on, and you'll learn of another member of the underworld whose *modus operandi* and fate are similar.

Overview of the Text

For better or worse, we have a fascination with the paranormal. We love to be frightened with terrible tales of demons and goblins. Whether it's a Ouija board at a teenage girl's slumber party or a casual read of the day's horoscope, this sort of "beyond the veil" stuff captures our imagination. From Frank Peretti to *Friday the 13th*, we love the goose bumps raised by the paranormal. Our present text tells such a story, only this one isn't fiction. The spirit world is all very real and very close. What this text teaches is that Jesus is Lord, even of the underworld.

Pondering the Power of Jesus

- In what way does Satan have hold of your heart and mind? What battles are you losing?
- Have you ever experienced spiritual warfare? What was it like?

- How are you preparing yourself for battle with Satan?
- Do you know of anyone who is demonized? What are they going through? How can you help them?

Meaning of the Text

Imagine a cross between Helen Keller and Charles Manson. He can't talk or see, and he's quite possibly deaf as well. He's shut off from the outside world, but the voices in his head rage. He lashes out in demonic fury. Terrified, alone, and confused, he is trapped inside a prison of deafening silence and hellish torment. Suddenly, the voices inside his head shriek as they fade into the distance. Light floods into his eyes. His head clears, his tongue is loosed, and he knows he is in his right mind once again.

A man stands before him. He's clearly a rabbi and an exorcist to boot, only his powers don't come from magical incantations or formulas. There were no burning candles, no ritual ceremonies, no prayers or petitions to dead ancestors. No, this one was different. He just ordered the demons out by his own moral authority. In an instant they fled without so much as an argument. The demoniac had to be extraordinarily grateful. Yet he never gets to express his thanks. For as soon as his sanity returns, he finds himself in the middle of a heated debate next to Jesus of Nazareth.

A group of vituperative Pharisees encircled them. Their bitterness splattered Jesus with accusations. "He's working for Beelzebub," they cried. What a horrible thing to say. Beelzebu*l* ("Lord of the house") was a Canaanite god. The Jews mocked Jesus by calling him Beelzebu*b*, meaning, "Lord of flies." It came to be an alternative title to Satan himself. They were saying Jesus was employed by Satan. In a sense, their response is understandable. Jesus has been winning the crowds with impressive miracles. The leaders have to either yield to him or stop him. If they are to stop him, they must come up with some explanation of his extraordinary power.

In those days everyone assumed the existence of a very interactive spirit world. Thus the accusations of some naturalistic trickery or psychosomatic healings were not really options. They can either say, "Jesus is from God," and follow him, or they can say, "Jesus is from the Devil, and you better watch out!"

Obviously, Jesus isn't going to take that one sitting down. His responses are fierce, immediate, and logical. First, "A house divided against itself can't stand" (v. 25). There is no way Satan is going to cast out demons. Could he? Sure. Would he? Not on your life! Thus, the suggestion that Jesus is Satan's envoy ultimately makes no sense.

Second, if Jesus' exorcism were by Satan, then wouldn't that explanation also apply to their own exorcists (v. 27)? Why would a pharisaic exorcist be of God and Jesus be from the Devil when they're doing pretty much the same thing? Is that possible? Theoretically, yes; practically, no.

Third, if we discount the Pharisees' explanation, there is only one possibility left—Jesus is from God. Listen to what Luke says. He replaces the word "Spirit of God" with "Finger of God," (v. 28; Luke 11:20). This is a unique phrase found only four times (NIV). Twice it refers to the tablets of stone which God inscribed with his finger and once it refers to the miracles of Moses which the Egyptian magicians were unable to imitate (Exod. 8:19). Now *that's* interesting! In this present context that's a powerful image. Jesus, like Moses, stands apart from all other magicians and exorcists. His works are qualitatively different—clearly the very finger of God enables him to perform such wonders.

Finally, Jesus says that their accusations border on blasphemy of the Holy Spirit. The Spirit of God empowered Jesus' wonders. To assign those deeds to the Devil is to accuse the Holy Spirit of being the unholy Spirit. That is inappropriate, unkind, and unsafe. How dare they scandalize the very person of Yahweh! Jesus retaliates with a threat, "You continue on this course and you'll not be forgiven." He continues with this curious comment, "You can say whatever you want about me, but blaspheme the Holy Spirit and you're dead!" Yikes! What gives here? Is Jesus like a defensive groom that threatens his bride's critics? Is he some soccer mom that comes unglued when the referee red cards her darling?

Why can we be forgiven if we criticize Jesus, but not if we blaspheme the Holy Spirit? Is he more sensitive? Does he get his feelings hurt easily? NO. The reason is simple. Think of it this way. God has been attempting to reach his humanity since the days of creation. He imbedded his fingerprints in the very earth on which we walk. He placed in our hearts a spirit that yearns for a relationship with its creator. He gave us the law to teach us about morality. He sent the prophets to speak to us about God's plan. Then came John the Baptist blazing a trail for the Messiah. Jesus preached like no other and healed, loved, and lived impeccably. All this evidence is strung along the history of our existence. The last and final evidence is the prompting of the Holy Spirit through the undeniable miracles of Jesus. It's like a rope with knots tied at intervals and draped over a cliff with a sheer and deep drop. If we miss the evidence of creation, there's another knot below. If we miss the law or prophets, there's always more to come. If we miss a sermon of Jesus, or even one of his miracles, there's still a chance. But if we reject the overpowering evidence of the Holy Spirit, we are doomed.

Listen, Jesus isn't speaking so harshly because he hates these men, but because he desperately wants to save them. At some point in a critical emergency one has to leave off coaxing and rush straight to a full-throttled shout. The sirens of salvation are blaring, the red warning lights are flashing: Repent or Perish!

Satan's Card House

Now what does all this mean for those who think they might have committed this sin against the Holy Spirit? The very fact that one is concerned about having blasphemed the Spirit is a sure indication that they have not. Why? Well, it is the very Spirit of God that convicts us of sin, righteousness, and judgment to come (John 16:8). Thus, one under conviction is still being worked on. Once the Spirit withdraws, we lose our ability to be drawn to the things of God. Remember, this blasphemy of the Spirit is not a slip of the tongue in a rash moment but a rejection of a lifetime of God's wooing. Those who feel compelled to know God are under conviction of the Spirit whom they've not yet ultimately rejected.

There is one more issue here to put on the table. If we brush aside all the curious details of blasphemy and the demonic, what does this text tell us about the nature of Christ? After all, it is not a tale about the paranormal but the person of Jesus. He is the unmitigated Lord, not only of the heavens and earth but of Satan's dark dominion as well. His relationship with the Father grants him authority over angels. His miracles on earth clearly show his control over the concrete. Yet this story tells of his superlative power over demons, even Satan himself. Jesus towers over all things, the seen and the unseen, the light and the dark, the angelic and demonic, the earthly, the heavenly, even the hellish. He is the incomparable, unconquerable Christ.

Participating in the Power of Jesus

Take an hour or two out of a day and retreat to a quiet place—possibly a park, a room in your home, your deck, just somewhere quiet. Take a notebook and a pen with you and spend some time in reflection on the previous year. Evaluate areas of weakness. Areas where Satan attacks on a regular basis and wins. Admit the weakness, the struggle to God in prayer, and ask him to help you develop a plan for overcoming them. Next, evaluate the areas where you have grown in the past year and spend time thanking God for those victories.

> Jesus Christ turns life right-side-up, and heaven outside-in.
> —Carl F. H. Henry

4

MASTER OF RAGING STORMS AND RAVING DEMONIACS

Text: Mark 4:35–5:20 **Memory:** Mark 4:39-41

Calm in the Storm

Charles is not your typical church greeter or usher. You wouldn't know it from his smile and from the kind words he shares, but his first encounter with the world was stormy to say the least. His parents had been anticipating his arrival the way most young couples anticipate a firstborn. So when the water broke and delivery was unavoidable, they called their doctor and asked him to come to their home. He was on vacation at the time and when he received the call he had been drinking. Angered that he had to leave the festivities early, he arrived at their home in a drunken fit of rage. He found Mrs. Gehlauf lying on a bed dealing with labor pains. Instead of allowing her to follow the natural course of child bearing, he decided to hurry things up so he could get back to his social hour. He climbed up on her bed, placed his knee in her stomach and pushed.

 Needless to say, there were complications. Charles was born with physical challenges that most of us cannot comprehend and his mother died in the process.

Elzie Gehlauf, Charles's father, buried his wife and began the difficult battle of raising a son whom most people thought would never learn to walk or talk. Every day for two years, Elzie carried Charles to a physical therapist. Charles is now in his 60s and I've known him my entire life. My family used to give him a ride to church every Sunday. That is, until Charles outgrew our family station wagon and needed the church van. You see, Charles talks. He expresses what is on the inside and because he does, the first row of my home church is filled with people Charles has led to the Lord. And not only does Charles talk, but he's even been known to sing.

I was maybe ten years of age when Charles struggled to make his way up the stairs to the stage. He stood in front of a microphone and though we had to strain to understand him, boy did he sing! And the song he sang was more than appropriate. He sang: "When the trumpet of the Lord shall sound and time shall be no more And the morning breaks eternal, bright, and fair, When the saved of earth shall gather over on the other shore And the roll is called up yonder, I'll be there."

And I've thought since, for a man who by worldly standards is considered limited, Charles understands that storms are temporary when you really know who Jesus is.

Overview of the Text

At the pinnacle of our text we find the crucial question: "Who is this?" (Mark 4:41). It springs from the terrified Twelve who see Jesus' power squelch a typhoon. They've followed him for the better part of a year, yet still have no clue whom they're dealing with. Stranger still, the answer to their question comes not from the inner band but from the lips of the Gerasene demoniac. He declares Jesus the "Son of the Most High God" (Mark 5:7). His spiritual storm is calmed, thus clarifying further the answer to this critical question, "Who is Jesus?" It's not just a question for the Twelve. It is the query of ages. Answer this and storms dissipate.

Pondering the Power of Jesus

- What was the most difficult thing you've ever had to go through? Did you know Jesus at the time? If so, how did the knowledge of his person help you through your tough time?
- What were some of the mistaken notions of Jesus' day about his identity? What do people mistake Jesus for today?
- How much "God" is Jesus? What kinds of things does he or will he do that demonstrate his divinity?

Meaning of the Text

Although this is the first time in Mark that Jesus has enacted his power over nature, we learn from John that he has already turned water into wine. Even so, that was mere sleight of hand compared to this. For one thing, no one's life was in jeopardy at the wedding (merely a groom's reputation). Peter & Co. know all too well the lethal power of these sudden storms. They were well aware of the boats at the bottom of this lake. When Jesus calmed the storm, he clearly crossed a line that opened their eyes. They've hailed him as Rabbi up until now. Suddenly they see he's treading where only Yahweh walks.

Before we get into the boat, however, we need to survey the landscape. This event takes place at the end of a very long day. It started with Jesus' family trying to apprehend him (Mark 3:20-21). They were convinced he was mentally unstable (which in those days was seen as a sign of demon possession). Next, Jesus exorcises a demoniac who was both blind and dumb (Mark 3:22-34). This led the Pharisees to accuse him of being Beelzebub's envoy rather than God's.

That was such a serious accusation that Jesus wheels around and warns them about blaspheming the Holy Spirit. Notice, however, that both the family and the Pharisees basically say the same thing of Jesus—he's demon possessed. Neither the Pharisees nor his family understand who Jesus is.

Then, after a long series of kingdom parables (Mark 4:1-34), Jesus and the boys head out to open waters where they encounter this storm (Mark 4:35-41). There in the middle of the lake, we discover that the disciples are nearly as ignorant of Jesus as the Pharisees and his own family. Watch what happens.

As the storm rages, Jesus sleeps. He's exhausted from a taxing day. Waves toss the boat back and forth, water splashes over the sides soaking everyone to the bone, and Jesus is out cold. The sailors man the oars; the landlubbers bail water from the boat. Finally one of the disciples wakes Jesus. Because we know the end of the story, our initial impulse is to interpret this as an act of faith. "Go get Jesus to save us." That can't be correct, however. For when Jesus does intervene and stills the storm, they are shocked. That is beyond anything they could have imagined. We're not exactly sure why they woke Jesus. Perhaps out of instinct, perhaps to provide leadership, but more likely it was simply a call for all hands on deck. Perhaps Iscariot needed his help to bail water from the boat. Can you imagine, Yahweh is in the boat and you ask him to help bail out water! It is amazing how they underutilized the access to God they had. Yet this scene is played out a thousand different ways in our own lives. Oh, our songs sing his praise, but our petitions deny his power.

Jesus stood up in the boat (a very foolish thing to do in a storm . . . unless, of course, you can walk on water). He ordered the forces of nature to shush. When they did, the disciples stood in paralyzed silence. Finally someone asked, probably in hushed tones on a placid lake, "Who is this? Even the wind and the waves obey him!" That is the critical question even still.

Jesus has a question of his own, equally important: "Do you still have no faith?" Now wait just a minute! It is one thing to follow Jesus as a prophet or even a miracle worker. But to acclaim him as God is a decidedly different thing. To trust him to stand before a hurricane and halt it with an outstretched hand is stretching our faith to the breaking point. Yet Jesus acts as if that would be the natural, even minimal response to his person and preaching. Frankly this text frightens me, for it demands more faith, I'm afraid, than I'm able to muster. Yet there sits Jesus' demand, relentless, even nonchalant.

Across the lake those watching the herd of pigs must be "weirded out." This storm dissipates as quickly as it came. From atop the cliffs these "sowboys" watch as a lone ship makes its way to shore after the treacherous storm. With interest they peer over the tombs, knowing that their local maniac would attack these unsuspecting Jews. It's a cheap thrill for the sowboys, bored out of their minds on the evening shift.

To their surprise the demoniac stops short of the rabbi. On his knees he pleads with Jesus to do him no harm. Remember, this is coming from a naked lunatic with self-inflicted scars; a man who screams, tears chains, chases the locals, and lives in tombs. The legion of demons (some 6,000 strong) request leave to enter the hogs. To the sowboys' consternation, permission was granted. The deviled ham went hog wild. They raced down the steeps into the lake committing SUIcide. The sowboys ran to town to call an emergency meeting. The major cash crop of the area had just been destroyed. This would decimate the economy of the eastern side of the lake.

When the owners of the herd arrived, they saw the man at Jesus' feet, dressed and in his right mind. They were furious and terrified. On the one hand, they were bitter about the loss. On the other hand, they were petrified by Jesus' power. They had tried to chain the man several times. Like an addict on PCP he tore the chains, doing bodily damage to himself and anyone he could get a hold of. But now, there he sits, like a well-trained lap dog. Who is this man who arrives through a deadly storm and orders about a legion of demons? They were terrified of Jesus, so they ask him to leave. As a gentleman, he does.

The demoniac, however, asks permission to follow him. That only makes sense. What kind of life would he have back in Gerasa? He was an embarrassment to his family, the ladies have all seen his scars, and what man in his right mind would hire him after the economic devastation he caused. He is a liability to the community. We expect Jesus to welcome such a one. He does not! Rather he sends him home with a simple message: "Go to your family and tell them how much the Lord has done for you, and how he has had mercy on you." With no other good options, the man obeys. Boy, does he obey! The next verse says he spread the news of Jesus through the entire Decapolis. Now that is not the city of Gerasa. Rather it is Gerasa plus nine other Greek cities of the vicinity. This man, with less than six hours of Bible College education, spread a simple story of Jesus' great power. While the disciples are still wrestling with the Master's identity, this Gentile ex-demoniac is spreading his fame. In fact, the next time Jesus comes around, they'll not ask him to leave. Instead, Jesus will feed 4,000 on this east side of the lake.

We're now ready to look at this text from the bird's-eye view. While Jesus' family and the Pharisees see Jesus as a demon-crazed lunatic, his own disciples aren't much ahead of them. Oh they follow him as rabbi, and they are certainly familiar with his uncanny ability to cast out demons and heal people. What they seem thoroughly unprepared for, however, is his true identity as God. We're not talking here about a magician or prophet. We're talking about a man who can calm storms and order around a legion of demons. He is, as the Gerasene lunatic said, "The Son of the Most High God." For our part, we might say many nice things about Jesus. We might believe noble things of him. But he's not come to be hailed as a nice guy or a mysterious wonder-worker. He's come to reveal his most startling identity—the very Son of God.

Participating in the Power of Jesus

Go to the nearest Bible book store and purchase these two books:

The Life You've Always Wanted **by John Ortberg**
Traveling Light **by Max Lucado**

5

LORD OVER BLOOD AND DEATH

> Preach to the suffering, and you will never lack a congregation. There is a broken heart in every pew.
>
> —Joseph Parker

Text: Mark 5:21-43 **Memory:** Mark 5:36

Forgiven! The name Norma McCorvey probably doesn't mean anything to you. But the pseudonym that Norma McCorvey used in the landmark Supreme Court case in which she was the plaintiff you will probably recognize—Jane Roe, of *Roe versus Wade,* the infamous decision in 1973 that legalized abortion on demand.

In 1969 Norma McCorvey was working as a barker for a traveling carnival when she discovered she was pregnant. She asked a doctor to give her an abortion and was surprised to find it was against the law. She sought help elsewhere and was recruited as the plaintiff in *Roe versus Wade* by two attorneys seeking to overturn the law against abortion. Ironically, because the case took some four years to be finally decided, McCorvey never was able to abort the child and instead gave her baby up for adoption.

She remained anonymous for a decade or so, and then Norma McCorvey went public, nervously telling a Dallas television reporter that she was Jane Roe of *Roe v. Wade*. For the first time publicly, she admitted she had lied about that pregnancy in the hope it would help her get an abortion. It was a casual affair that made her pregnant, not rape as she told her Roe lawyers. And, little by little, through occasional interviews, sporadic speaking engagements, and a 1989 television movie, she revealed that before she gave birth to the Roe baby and gave her to adoptive parents, she had given birth to two other children.

According to writer Jeff Hooten in *Citizen*, McCorvey soon went to work answering phones for a Dallas abortion clinic. Next door to the clinic was a pro-life office facility. After a time, Norma began to have a change of heart. Hooten writes that her turning point came when a 7-year-old girl named Emily—the daughter of a pro-life volunteer who greeted McCorvey each day with a hug—invited McCorvey to church. On July 22, 1995, McCorvey attended a Saturday night church service in Dallas. "Norma just kept praying, 'I want to undo all the evil I've done in this world,'" said Ronda Mackey, Emily's mother. In August of 1995 she was baptized in a swimming pool in front of ABC "World News Tonight" television cameras. Says McCorvey, "I still feel very badly. I guess I always will . . . but I know I've been forgiven."

Only Jesus can shine through the darkness of sin. Only Jesus can shine through the pain of suffering.

Overview of the Text

We have here a pair of miracles, both wrought for women. One is a girl in the flower of her youth, just twelve years old. The other woman has been bleeding the entire time the girl has been alive. Both are in desperate straits. On the surface, their testimony speaks of Jesus' power to heal as well as his compassion for women. That's certainly nothing to sneeze at. However, if we step back and view them from the shadow of the cross something larger comes into view. Their stories, clearly connected by the number twelve, tell not of what Jesus did for two so long ago, but what he does for us all through Calvary. These ladies stand as mirrors of our own plight. Jesus, through his own blood and death, cures us of our perilous ills.

Pondering the Power of Jesus

- Have you ever had someone announce to you the death of a loved one? Describe how it happened and how you felt.
- Have you ever felt like an outsider? What made you feel like one and how did you respond to the situation?
- What does Jairus risk in coming to Jesus? What did/would it "cost" you to become a follower of Jesus and ask for his help in your plight of life?

Meaning of the Text

He's just returned from Gerasa. With little sleep, and no mention of food, Jesus arrives at Capernaum exhausted and hungry. But there'll be no rest for the weary. He's mobbed as soon as he sets foot from the boat. Everyone wants to touch him, see him, and hear him. Two individuals in particular will win the day.

Jairus is able to make his way through the crowd due to his clout. He is the ruler of the local synagogue and able to go pretty much wherever he wants. It is not surprising that he is ushered to the front of the line. What is surprising, however, is that he wants to be there. You see, just yesterday, Jesus and the Pharisees had a blowout. He healed a blind-dumb demoniac, and the Pharisees accused him of doing it by the power of the Devil. Jesus lashed back with threatening words about the blasphemy of the Holy Spirit. Jesus and the religious establishment are not getting along so well just now. But Jairus is desperate. His only child, a girl, is on her deathbed. He has nowhere else to turn, and the girl has apparently taken a turn for the worse since yesterday when Jesus was in town to teach. He comes with a desperate appeal. Jesus agrees to help and the parade to Jairus's house begins.

On the way, however, something curious happened. One of the locals had been bleeding for twelve years. This is apparently a gynecological problem. For her it is worse than mere embarrassment. As a Jewess, this condition made her unclean. It separated her from the synagogue, from her husband, and from social interaction. Everything she touched was unclean so she became a pariah. To exacerbate the problem, the hygienic conditions of her day made it impossible to hide. Every day she would have to take her menstrual cloths to the water's edge and clean them. Moreover, without sanitary cleansing and disposal she would begin to stink. This wouldn't be as offensive in their culture as it is in ours. They're used to lots of animals and sweaty workers with few showers and no air conditioning. However, her odor would be an olfactory reminder of her uncleanness. As she approaches Jesus from behind, the other peasants get a whiff and step aside.

Mark simply says, "She touched his cloak." We can probably be a bit more specific. Every Jewish male wore a prayer shawl. At each corner were tassels with specific knots tied along their length. These knots represented prayers. They worked like rosary beads. As the rabbi ran down the trail of knots on the tassel, he would pray a prayer for each. The talk of the day was that the more powerful the rabbi the more powerful his prayers. Furthermore, they believed that a "residue" of this prayer power remained in the tassels he'd fingered. By touching them, the woman was hoping to access the power of his prayers. Superstitious? Probably. Effective? Absolutely. She felt a surge through her body that told her instantly that her decade-plus problem was solved. Just as quickly, however, Jesus stopped in his tracks and said, "Someone touched me." Well, of course they had touched him—he's being swarmed. The closest in the crowd, however, still denied it. Peter couldn't believe it: "Master, the whole crowd is mobbing you!" (Luke 8:45). Jesus somehow sensed that power went forth from him into this woman. He turns to find out who it was. She's not hard to spot. She's the one cowering and quivering! She comes clean about the cleansing, and Jesus announces to the crowd that her physical problem is solved and thus her social isolation is over. While this may be uncomfortable to talk about publicly, it was important for her neighbors to know that she now has open access to the community once again. No doubt spontaneous jubilation erupted. The crowd goes wild . . . except for Jairus. He's standing nervously to the side tapping his Rolex.

Just then his servants arrive with some very bad news. "Your daughter is dead; don't bother the Master any more." Bummer. Their announcement is rather brusque. With a rude emphasis on his daughter's condition, they literally told Jairus, "DEAD your daughter is." It must have hit him like a ton of bricks. Immediately Jesus jumps in front of a dazed Jairus and says, "Don't be afraid; just believe, and she will be healed." His head is spinning but he staggers on toward his house.

As they arrive, they hear the sound of flutes, a sure sign that a funeral is in progress. The whole entourage is there—mourners, musicians, pall bearers. Jesus tells them to go home because she is only asleep. Their mourning turns to mocking in an instant. Jesus is the brunt of their jeers, but he'll have the last laugh. Jesus kicks everyone out of the house save Jairus and his wife and his own inner three. He takes the girl by the hand and tells her to get up. She does. We want to pause here and marvel at such a majestic miracle, but there is no time. The story line races on. Jesus tells her parents to give her something to eat (clear evidence that she was, in fact, a teenager). Eating was a social sign of solidarity. In other words, the girl is not just brought back from the dead, but truly reincorporated into the family. This is similar to what Jesus did for the woman who was bleeding when he reinstated her back into the community.

Then Jesus says something that is truly bizarre. He tells

Jairus and his wife not to talk about what happened. Oh, Jesus has his reasons. He's already so popular that he can't safely walk the streets of Capernaum. Misconceptions are running amuck and misleading advertising is the last thing Jesus needs. Nevertheless, asking a father not to talk about the resuscitation of his only child is too much to hope for. Besides, the attendees of the funeral are going to demand some kind of explanation.

Now here we have two extraordinary miracles. They stand in tandem across the number 12, telling of Christ's great power to heal. Yet there is a subtext that runs through these two stories all the way to Calvary. The fact that all three synoptics (Matthew, Mark, and Luke) tell of these events indicates their importance. Something significant is happening here. We have an older woman whose problem was blood. Next to her is a young girl whose problem is death. Place them next to each other and answer this question: When else are blood and death connected in the Gospels? It is when Jesus himself unites the two in his own body. These women foreshadow the work of Christ on the cross. They stand as mirrors of our own predicament—defilement, isolation, and shame. They show how Jesus takes the worst we have to offer and undoes the work of the Devil. He takes our sickness upon himself and reinstates us to the community of God's people. Only this time, we can talk about it all we want.

Participating in the Power of Jesus

Oftentimes homeless people represent the outskirts of society. Fringe people who are often misunderstood for one reason or another, they are left alone in many communities to continue in dangerous cycles of drug abuse, prostitution, and violence. Take an afternoon and spend some time at a local homeless shelter. Volunteer to feed or visit with those who come in. Record your experiences and conversations in a journal. And from time to time, revisit the shelter and your journal.

Lord over Blood and Death

6 HAIL TO THE CHIEF

The true function of a preacher is to disturb the comfortable and to comfort the disturbed.

—Chad Walsh

Surely the preacher's greatest sin is to put people to sleep with the greatest story ever told.

—Bruce W. Thielemann

Actors speak of things imaginary as if they were real, while you preachers too often speak of things real as if they were imaginary.

—Thomas Betterton

When power goes out of the message, it is because the Word has become not flesh, but words.

—Leighton Ford

Text: Matthew 10:1-42 **Memory:** Matthew 10:27-31

Spread the Word! An auto body shop may seem like an unlikely location for a sermon to be preached. But stranger things have happened, and I suppose it depends on how we define a sermon. But it was in a business where damaged cars are repaired that a twelve-year-old boy named Scott learned that the damaged areas of his life could be permanently fixed. Sandblasting, replacing totaled or dented areas, and applying fresh coats of paint are not foreign tasks to God.

An elder in our church owns the business and takes the responsibility of preaching seriously, so he shared one day with Scott, whose dad works in the shop, what Jesus had been doing in his life. Scott lived next door to a family that frequently shared that same message, so he reasoned in his heart and mind that God was calling him to make some changes. So Scott surrendered, accepted Jesus as Lord and Savior, and was baptized. And he lived out what he had seen. He didn't have a Bible college education, he wasn't well versed in apologetics. He simply knew Jesus. He shared what he knew with his mom, and a year later, Scott's mom Kathy decided her life was in need of God's skill and expertise, a restoration if you will. Appropriately, at the age of 13, Scott baptized his mom. And on the baptism certificate where a minister generally signs, Scott Welch inscribed his name.

Overview of the Text

Twice Jesus sends out his disciples to preach. The first time he commissions the Twelve up in Galilee (Matt. 10); the second time he sends out the seventy down in Judea (Luke 10). Obviously they are valuable help in announcing the kingdom. They can go many more places than Jesus alone. Yet something else comes to the surface as the two groups stand side by side. Twelve is a symbolic number. It represents the number of the tribes of Israel. Thus, when Jesus installs twelve Apostles, they stand as potential leaders of the twelve tribes as Jesus inaugurates his rule over a new nation. The Seventy mirror the number of members in the Sanhedrin. This supreme court over Israel was the highest legislative body in the land. Jesus' delegates are prepared to represent his rule in the soon-coming kingdom. Jesus stands as king. The Twelve are his cabinet. The seventy represent the judiciary. All the administrative structure is in place for a new nation to rise. No wonder the current political rulers of Israel got so nervous about Jesus' program. In fact, this is brassy enough that it requires a lethal response to squelch.

Pondering the Power of Jesus

- In your estimation, what is the job of a preacher? If you were to draw up a job description, what kinds of things would you put on it? Is it dangerous work?

Hail to the Chief

- ☧ What could you, or would you, be willing to do to help your preacher carry out his commission for Christ?
- ☧ Have you ever been called to "preach"? What have you been commissioned by God to do to propagate this message of the kingdom? What is your role in this enterprise called "The Church"?

Meaning of the Text

Read through both chapters (Matt. 10 & Luke 10) and fill out the following chart. You are looking for all the similarities (and differences) between the two commission accounts:

Matthew	Luke	Similarities/Differences
10:1-2	10:1	12 / 70
9:37-38	10:2	same harvest few labourers
10:16	10:3	same – lambs among wolves
10:8-10	10:4	heal sick, same – Carry nothing c̄ you
10:11-13	10:5-8	same –
10:7-8	10:9	same – kingdom is at hand
10:14-15	10:10-12	same – shake off dust
10:40-42	10:16	same – whoever rec. you rec me
11:1 (cf. Mk 6:30)	10:17-20	return to Jesus rejoicing – "I gave you power"

According to this chart, those commissioned by Christ to preach have several functions. These make a pretty good model for modern ministry. While there may be a thousand different details your local preacher needs to administrate, all the essential ones fall under four umbrellas.

First, **we, as preachers, are to announce the good news of the kingdom.** It's really a blast. Preachers get to tell people the best stuff. To be sure, there is that ugly announcement of sin and that uncomfortable warning of hell. But once we get past that we get to tell people about the grace of God, forgiveness of sins, the fellowship of the Holy Spirit, the community of believers, gifts of service, transformation, and a trilogy of a new heaven, new earth, and a new body. That'll make you sing! This has to be the greatest job in the world—going around and telling people that while they were once God's enemy, they can now become his friend. Even more, they can become an adopted child, precious beyond imagination.

Second, **we heal people.** The Apostles, of course, had miraculous powers to heal all sorts of diseases as well as demon possession. Today those gifts are dispersed more broadly. Some have the gift of healing. Others spend years in medical school. Some master power encounters while others become adept counselors. There is a plethora of ways Christ's ambassadors bring healing today—mind, body, and soul. He is still in the business of putting Humpty-Dumpties back together again. Yet this healing needs to be put in perspective. Obviously, everyone who has ever been healed physically eventually died. Thus, physical healing of this body is not God's ultimate purpose for us. Rather, it is a picture, a prediction, of what he promises. It is a sign of heaven and a symbol of the power of Jesus over the work of the Devil. You see, Satan scours the earth looking for people to oppress. Jesus and his delegates meandered from place to place thwarting the work of the evil one.

The bottom line of these healing powers is *authority*. When Christ calls us, he empowers us to undo the work of the Devil at every level. In fact, that's what is meant by giving a blessing to homes we enter (Luke 10:5-7). We actually have God's authority to pronounce blessings on those worthy. God invests so much authority in us that our hosts are actually blessed by our presence. Conversely, when a community rejects the word, we have the authority to curse that community (Luke 10:10-15). No, no, no, this is not like voodoo or witchcraft. It is like what Jesus did when he pronounced prophetic doom on Capernaum, Korazin, and Bethsaida (cf. Matt. 11:21-21). It is the shaking of dust and an imprecatory prayer against those who reject the gospel. This is no temper tantrum for a personal offense but an announcement of God's judgment on the recalcitrant heart. We heal (and curse), thus extending Jesus' kingdom authority to every place we set our feet.

Third, we endure persecution. Matthew actually has a lot to say about this that Luke doesn't record (Matt. 10:16-25). We will stand before civic courts and religious leaders. We will be beaten by police, soldiers, even members of our own family. We will experience physical abuse such as beatings, floggings, and imprisonment as well as verbal abuse through slander, lies, and libel. Obviously this does not mean that every Christian is destined to experience the entire range of these sufferings. But as a general rule, the more one preaches and the more new territory one claims, the more likely (even inevitable) is one's opposition.

Fourth, we receive a reward. The question is, why would a person want to subject herself to torture? Matthew addresses this issue (Matt. 10:26-33). In short, he gives four reasons: (1) The truth will eventually be obvious to everyone (vv. 26-27). At that point you want to make sure you're on the right side. (2) God is not to be trifled with (v. 28). It is wiser to fear God's punishment of hell than the persecution of men. (3) God loves you with unparalleled precision and detail, even down to the number of hairs on your head (vv. 29-31). He's not going to let things get out of his control. (4) There is great reward for those who accept the commission to preach. Jesus will acknowledge us before the Father in heaven (v. 32). By losing our life we will gain it (v. 39). Not only does God lavish blessings on us, but even those who host the preacher will receive a permanent reward (v. 40-42). Many have noted that preachers are often underpaid. Sometimes that's true. Businessmen, doctors, lawyers, and other professionals make much more money as a general rule. But let's not forget the retirement plan; for the preacher it's out of this world!

Let's revisit our introduction. We have a group of 12 and 70, both portraying political branches of Jesus' new government. They are charged with responsibility and endowed with authority. While the social setting has changed and the job description has morphed just a bit, the basic commission is still the same. Those who preach the gospel are not merely educators or evangelists. They are leaders in the kingdom of God, charged with propagating the message and implementing God's reign on this earth.

Participating in the Power of Jesus

Set aside the time this week to write two letters. Write the first letter to the person who led you to Christ. Thank that person for his or her prayers, encouragement, patience, and ability to communicate the person of Jesus to you. Write the second letter to a preacher you listen to every Sunday and thank him for the labor of love he brings to the stage each week.

7 7

LORD OF ALL CREATION

7 7

> Full-grown oaks are not produced in three years; neither are servants of God.
>
> —Douglas Rumford
>
> Faith is not belief without proof but trust without reservation.
>
> —Elton Trueblood
>
> Hope is hearing the melody of the future. Faith is to dance to it!
>
> —Rubem Alves

Text: Matthew 14:13-36 **Memory:** Matthew 14:35-36

The Perfect Timepiece

In the town hall in Copenhagen stands the world's most complicated clock. It took forty years to build at a cost of more than a million dollars. That clock has ten faces, fifteen thousand parts, and is accurate to two-fifths of a second every three hundred years. The clock computes the time of day, the days of the week, the months and years, and the movements of the planets for twenty-five hundred years. Some parts of that clock will not move until twenty-five centuries have passed.

What is intriguing about that clock is that it is still not accurate. It loses two-fifths of a second every three hundred years. Like all clocks, the timepiece in Copenhagen must be regulated by a more precise clock, the universe itself. That mighty astronomical clock with its billions of moving parts from atoms to stars, rolls on century after century with movements so reliable that all time on earth can be measured against it.

At the speed of light, 186,000 miles a second, sunlight takes eight minutes to reach the earth. That same light takes five more hours to reach Pluto, the farthest planet in our solar system. After leaving our solar system that same sunlight must travel for four years and four months to reach the next star in the universe. That is a distance of 40 trillion kilometers. The sun resides in the Milky Way Galaxy, which is home to hundreds of billions of stars. The sun is small in comparison to many of the stars in this system! Yet, the Milky Way is but one of roughly one trillion galaxies in the universe. Says astronomer Allan Sandage, "Galaxies are to astronomy what atoms are to physics." Astronomers estimate that the distance across the universe is roughly 40 billion light-years and that there are roughly 100 billion trillion stars.

Is it unreasonable to think that Jesus could feed a few thousand people or walk on the surface of a lake? Read on, and you be the judge!

Overview of the Text

The feeding of the 5,000 and Jesus' walking on water stand as twin towers over the question of his identity. As we trace the contours of Jesus' recent ministry, we find not a soul who really knows who this man is. Herod thinks he's John the Baptist reincarnated. John's disciples have serious reservations about following him as Messiah but now have nowhere else to turn with their leader's recent execution. The crowds just love him, but only like children who revere Santa for all the goodies he brings. Even his own disciples mistake him for a soon-coming king through a social uprising. Nobody knows him. So he begins to unfold his identity, not through words so easily misunderstood and forgotten, but through undeniably clear actions. He will act in this scene like the creator God we now know him to be (cf. John 1:1-4; Col. 1:15-17). He will generate from five small loaves enough to feed a hungry throng using nothing but the power of his will. He will hover over the turbulent waters just as the Spirit of God did at creation (Gen 1:2). From turbulent chaos he will create calm, and we will stand to take notice.

Pondering the Power of Jesus

- What is your favorite natural wonder? (Mountains, ocean, stars, etc.)
- Do you have a favorite season of the year?
- Do you daily thank God for the created world around you?
- Do you ever fall prey to worshiping the created over the Creator?
- If you could script a miracle involving Jesus and the natural wonder you mentioned above, what would the miracle look like? Who would be there? What would be the result?

Meaning of the Text

The Twelve returned from their first solo flight with a flurry of excited tales. They played "Can You Top This?" with accounts of exorcisms, healings, revivals, and sermons that brought ever increasing crowds to their feet. Surely Jesus listened with joy, his head thrown back in a full-throated belly laugh.

About the same time, however, another group of disciples came to Jesus. These were from John the Baptist. They came to report the chilling news of his gruesome execution. Surely Jesus was devastated. If he cried at the funeral of his friend Lazarus whom he knew he could raise, how he must have wailed over John, his forerunner and fellow steward of the incoming kingdom.

So what do you do in the face of triumph and tragedy? Well, a little R & R seems to be in order. So Jesus gathers the boys in the boat and they head to the far side of the lake. They travel from the southwest shore near Tiberias to the northeast side by Bethsaida. Some of the locals see him take off and pursue him on foot. That's right. They take off in a dead run along the shore of the lake. Stopping at each little dock they ask, "Is Jesus here?" As soon as they hear a "no," off again they go in a sprint to the next little villa in search of Jesus in flight. They run some 8-10 miles before they finally catch up with him. In fact, many arrive on the far shore before Jesus' boat even docked. Hundreds more trail behind. Some were slowed by age, others by the cots they carried in hopes that Jesus could help their loved ones.

There is Jesus, exhausted, emotionally wounded, hungry, frustrated. . . . There stand the crowds with long wish lists and pleading eyes. It's as if they have their umbilical cords in their hands waiting to plug them into Jesus to suck the very life from him. How does he respond? What will he do? Mark (6:34) records the truly astounding scene: "When Jesus landed and saw a large crowd, he had compassion on them, because they were like sheep without a shepherd. So he began teaching them many things."

His teaching gives way to healing and his healings last the bulk of the day. Evening approaches so the disciples suggest the crowds be sent away. In a surprising twist, Jesus orders the Twelve to feed them. Philip, the CPA of the group, rattles through some quick calculations, "Lord, that would require eight month's wages" (Mark 6:37). Undoubtedly Iscariot gets quite fidgety at this point. "Well, go see what we have to work with," Jesus orders. Before long, Andrew returns with a little boy and his sack lunch. It is slim pickings. All he has are five little barley loaves and two small fish. Now these barley loaves were like miniature pita bread only not so thick. Moreover, they're made from barley (the poor man's fare), rather than wheat. The fish were probably pickled and about the size of a sardine. From that Jesus feeds five thousand men, plus women and children—a crowd upwards of 15,000. The rejoicing is rampant, not merely because of a free lunch, but because they have found their Messiah. Ralph Waldo Emerson once wrote, "The sky is the daily bread of the eyes." And Jesus? He is the daily bread of our souls!

Many of these folk were on their way to the Passover in Jerusalem and were all too willing to escort Jesus to the throne. Herod wouldn't like it much but it would be a boon for the general population! They were so intent, in fact, that John says they were ready to make Jesus king by force (John 6:15). Only with difficulty did Jesus dissuade them. He sent the disciples off in a boat, much to their chagrin. He ordered the crowds to go on to find lodging for the evening and he went up alone into the hills to pray. This is somewhat noteworthy given the fact that Jesus started the day so exhausted that he tried to avoid the crowds. Then rather than sleeping he labored through the night on his knees.

About three in the morning he's finally finished. It's time to catch up with the Twelve. They still haven't made it to the other side of the lake. They've been struggling at the oars since he dismissed them, likely 5-6 hours earlier. They were disgruntled and discouraged when they left because they felt that Jesus was not stepping up to the plate when his destiny was at hand. Now they're in worse shape than when they left—exhausted, frightened, soaked, and cold. Suddenly they see Jesus walking on the water. You really can't blame them for not recognizing him. It's dark, they're worn out, and the headwind is spewing waves across the bow. Nor can you blame them for interpreting this apparition as a ghost—probably even the grim reaper! After all, who would have guessed that Jesus (even one who could calm a storm), would catch up to them by this particular short cut?!

Jesus comforts them by saying, "Stop being afraid. It is I." Well, that's quite nice. No, actually, it's astounding.

Imbedded in these two short sentences are a couple of pretty deep allusions. First, "Don't be afraid" is a phrase most often found on the lips of divine messengers. It's what angels say to humans when their jaws hit the floor and their knees start to knock. There is something about Jesus here that is "heavenly." Second, "It is I," if translated back into Hebrew would be "Yahweh." Obviously we don't want to make too much of this phrase. After all, it is used all the time simply to say, "It is I" without any kind of allusions to deity. Nonetheless, in this particular context, what with the water walking and all, it does seem that Jesus is making a claim to be Yahweh God. More on this to come.

Peter, having one of his classic moments, invites Jesus to prove himself by inviting Peter to join him amid the waves. He does. The results: Peter both wins the nonincarnate water walking record ***and*** proves how bunglesome he can be. His eyes shift from Jesus to the waves and down he goes. Jesus grabs him by the hand and raises him up. (Peter looks so much like us!) Both make their way back into the boat. As if all this isn't extraordinary enough, instantly the storm dissipates and the boat is docked. End of story, beginning of application.

There are two themes coursing through this text. First, Jesus is God. At the peak of his popularity he is badly misunderstood. Herod thinks he's John reincarnated; the disciples take him for a rebel king; and the crowds follow the standard Messianic militaristic line. In two dramatic acts of deity, Jesus proves who he is. He creates, like God did in the beginning, and he hovers over the waters as did the Spirit. That's lesson number one. Lesson number two pertains to the disciples, particularly Peter. This impetuous follower looks a lot like us. In fact, in the next four chapters Matthew will trace Peter's righthearted, wrongheaded failures in a sidebar of the narrative. Five different times Peter attempts to follow Jesus but fails, finding himself on the other side of a pretty stiff rebuke.

Matthew doesn't do this to mock his comrade. On the contrary, he does this to encourage us. Peter is held up as a mirror to our own quest for Christ. We want so desperately to know, follow, and honor Jesus. Yet storms come, winds blow. We want to get out of the boat, but we have such a time keeping our eyes on the Master.

As we lay these two lessons side by side we see a single focus. We are to imitate Peter but also learn from his mistakes. His problem was not merely that he didn't look to Jesus but that he didn't see him clearly. The Lord is not merely a Messiah or miracle worker. He is the living God. If we can just get him into clear focus, we'll see the storm suddenly dissipate and the boat arrive safely ashore.

Participating in the Power of Jesus

Plan your next vacation enjoying the world God has created. Set aside one day of your vacation to spend in solitude. Spend that day in worship, simply thanking God for what he has made. Take pictures, write in your journal, record the experience in some way so that you can revisit it from time to time.

> Out in front of us is the drama of men and of nations, seething, struggling, laboring, dying . . . but within the silences of the souls of men an eternal drama is ever being enacted . . . On the outcome of this inner drama rests, ultimately, the outer pageant of history.
>
> —Thomas Kelly

8 8

UNWASHED HANDS AND A NEW VIEW OF HUMANITY

8 8

Text: Matthew 15:1-20 **Memory:** Matthew 15:17-20

From the Heart

In September 1993, with the major league baseball season nearing its end, the first-place Philadelphia Phillies visited the second-place Montreal Expos.

In the first game of the series, the home team Expos came to bat one inning, trailing 7–4. Their first two batters reached base. The manager sent a pinch hitter to the plate, rookie Curtis Pride, who had never gotten a hit in the major leagues. Pride took his warm-up swings, walked to the plate, and on the first pitch laced a double, scoring two runners.

The stadium thundered as 45,757 fans screamed their approval. The Expos' third base coach called time, walked toward Pride, and told him to take off his batting helmet.

What's wrong with my helmet? wondered the rookie. Then, realizing what his coach meant, Pride tipped his cap to the appreciative fans.

After the game, someone asked Pride if he could hear the cheering. This person wasn't giving the rookie a hard time. Curtis Pride is 95 percent deaf.

"Here," Pride said, pointing to his heart. "I could hear it here."

In the same way, it is in the heart, that Jesus' message needs to find its home.

Overview of the Text

It seems like such a trivial issue. After all, what's the big deal about eating without washing your hands? Oh sure, Mom used to make a federal case out of it, but we all knew that grub around a campfire never killed anyone. So why attack Jesus over a trivial issue like this? Actually, the issue here is not hygiene but humanity. Washing of hands was not for cleanliness but godliness (and in this case they are *not* next to each other). It was a way of separating oneself from the unclean heathen. If you can't even eat with someone, it would be pretty difficult to have a relationship with them. When Jesus dismissed the dietary codes along with the rabbinic rules of cleansing, he was opening a Pandora's box of free association with all sorts of people.

Pondering the Power of Jesus

- What church tradition are you holding on to that prevents you from reaching out to those who do not have a relationship with Jesus yet?
- Is there a recognizable generational gap in the church you attend? What practical steps could be taken to bridge those differences?
- Over the years, has your heart hardened or softened towards those who do not have a relationship with Jesus yet? Do you struggle with judging the lost?

Meaning of the Text

The rules were very clear. Before you could eat a kosher meal, you had to wash your hands. In fact, there was even a certain *way* one was to wash. You must point your fingers up and pour at least a half an eggshell of water over them so as to completely cover the hand down to the wrist. The hands were then rubbed vigorously. You could use your other fist (so long as it had already been washed), or your forehead, or even a wall. If, however, you had been out and about where you would likely have come in contact with a Gentile, even this washing wasn't enough. You must wash each hand again, this time with the fingers pointing down. This allows the water that washed the defilement off your hand in the first place to be rinsed from the hand lest it contaminate the food that you put in your mouth.

The idea is not so far from us really. If we go back to the third grade playground we will remember well those invisible, but very real entities called "cooties." If a girl (or boy, as the case may be), touched you (or, God forbid, *kissed* you), you were obliged by your peers to cleanse yourself either by wiping vigorously or washing in the drinking fountain. Now we see this simply as immature imagination. For the Jews, however, it was not merely imagination but ritualistic reality. They were surrounded by foreign nations whose very encroachment threatened their unique identity. It was therefore paramount for them to differentiate themselves from other nations. One of the ways they had done this was through certain codes surrounding their tables. The Jewish prohibition against pork is probably the most well known. That one comes straight from the OT. But where does one find washing before meals in the pages of the Torah? Actually, we don't. Oh, there are certain passages like Leviticus 15:11 directing certain washings for bodily emissions. But this hand-washing ordinance was a rule made up by the rabbis (perhaps extrapolating from other washing regulations). When Jesus refuses to follow it, he is for sure running counter to culture. He is not, however, violating God's law.

Unwashed Hands and a New View of Humanity

These Pharisees have come all the way from Jerusalem to pick a fight with Jesus and he'll not disappoint them. When they question him about abandoning tradition, he accuses them of setting aside the word of God! Whoa, wait just a minute. How can he seriously suggest that these religious leaders, persnickety in their clerical duties, would blatantly ignore a command of God? He's going to have to come up with some *very* clear evidence to substantiate that accusation. He does. One of the most revered and significant laws of God is to honor one's parents. Paul, in fact, says it's the first commandment with a promise (Eph. 6:2), and its violation carried the death penalty under the Old Covenant. I would say that's a pretty important law! Yet it was set aside through the tradition of Corban. Put simply, Corban says that your ultimate obligation is to God. So far so good. But Corban went on to argue that if something is devoted to God, it could not be given to anyone else. Thus Pharisees were devoting their homes, land, wealth, etc. to God and when their parents needed their help they could refuse since their resources were devoted to God and thus "off limits." Here's the catch: One could devote these things to God upon his death. Thus, your resources are still at your disposal and off limits to anyone else. Sneaky. Ungodly! Jesus rightly charged them with hypocrisy (which is really quite humorous since hypocrites were literally Greek actors who wore a mask—Jesus was accusing them of being actors when their holier-than-thou attitude kept them from even entering the theater!).

According to the Reuters news agency, at the Galveston County Fair and Rodeo, a steer named Husker, weighing in at 1,190 pounds, was named grand champion. The steer was sold at an auction for $13,500 and slaughtered a few days after the competition. When veterinarians examined the carcass they found something suspicious. They discovered evidence of what is called "airing." To give steers a better appearance, competitors have been known to inject air into their animals' hides with a bicycle pump and a syringe. There is really no difference in the persona the Pharisees presented to the public than that of Husker and his owners who were guilty of "airing."

Let's step back and look at where we've been. The Pharisees said that defilement moved from one's hand through the mouth and into heart. Jesus reverses the arrangement (vv. 11 & 17-18). He argues that defilement begins with the *heart* and comes out our *mouth* and eventually winds up on our *hands*. Oh, that made the Pharisees mad. When Peter pointed out their ire, the Lord simply said, "Don't you worry about those people. God will uproot them." Not only did Jesus disregard their rules for washing, he dismissed the very ones who made the rules. They were dangerous, and Jesus said to have nothing to do with them. Twenty centuries later that's easy for us but for the Twelve, that would be earth shattering. These men were the revered leaders of their religious traditions. Were they simply to disregard their upbringing? Apparently so.

So what should we make of all this? Well, the obvious application is that righteousness is not a matter of external observance, rather it is an issue of one's heart. We can wash our hands in the right way, go to church, say our prayers, have our quiet times, and still have a wretched heart. Righteousness is an inside-out proposition. Our external behaviors don't create godly character. The best they can do is reveal it.

There is another application that is more subtle and, indeed, more important. For this we need to listen to Mark's conclusion to this text (Mark 7:19). In a little parenthetical comment he states, "In saying this, Jesus declared all foods clean." Against the backdrop of Cornelius's conversion in Acts 10:10-16,28 this is obviously not about food but people. You see, these dietary codes were means by which outsiders were excluded from table fellowship. If you can't eat with someone, it is difficult to have a relationship with them. When Jesus declared all foods clean, he enabled Jewish evangelists to spread the good news to Gentiles. Jesus isn't simply brushing aside a meaningless ritual; he is altering the very contours of the people of God. Now they can come in all shapes and sizes.

We rejoice, with our lips, over God's inclusiveness in Christ. Our lives, however, tell a different story. Are we really any more "welcoming" than the Pharisees? Don't we too have our religious stipulations which function as barriers to inclusion? You know, those rules we invented that are additions to the Bible: dress codes for church, taboos against drinking and tobacco, rules for listening to music and church attendance, scandalous glances at tattoos, piercings, and hair styles, (etc. *ad nauseum*). These "regulations" are intended to keep us pure. Perhaps they do. But they also keep us isolated from the very people who most need the love of Christ. There's nothing wrong with a personal (or even corporate) quest for righteousness. This is to be lauded. Yet we must never confuse our own human construction of moral regulations with the commands of Scripture. When we do, we tend to look righteous to one another but hypocritical both to a watching world and a weeping God.

Participating in the Power of Jesus

Be intentional about reaching out. Start by having an "Open Chair" policy in your small group or Sunday school class. Have an empty chair at each meeting to signify the person your group is yet to reach. Pray for the person, and when you fill that chair, add another empty chair to the group. When your group grows to capacity, birth a new group, always maintaining an open chair policy.

Resolved: that all men should live for the glory of God. Resolved second: that whether others do or not, I will.

—*Jonathan Edwards*

Attempt great things for God. Expect great things from God.

—*William Carey*

Courage is being scared to death but saddling up anyway.

—*John Wayne*

9 9

TRANSFIGURATION: GOD IN THE FLESH

9 9

Text: Matthew 17:1-13 **Memory:** Matthew 17:11-13

One of Us, but Not

The story is told of Shah Abbis, a Persian monarch who loved his people very much. To know them better, he would mingle with his subjects in various disguises.

One day he went dressed as a poor man to the public baths and in a tiny cellar sat beside the fireman who tended the furnace. When it was mealtime, the monarch shared the poor man's coarse food and talked to his lonely subject as a friend would. Again and again Shah Abbis visited the poor man and grew to love him as a brother. One day Shah Abbis revealed his true identity. It was common for people to ask for gifts or favors from the monarch, and that was what he expected from this poor furnace worker. But the poor man sat gazing at his ruler with love and wonder and at last spoke, "You left your palace to sit with me in this cold, dark place, to eat my coarse food, to care whether my heart is glad or sorry. On others you may bestow rich presents, but to me you have given yourself, and it only remains for me to pray that you never withdraw the gift of friendship."

Shah Abbis wasn't the first monarch to leave his throne, live among a common people, and love them as brothers.

Overview of the Text

Throughout the years of incarnation, this is the closest Jesus ever came to disrobing his humanity. The transfiguration is the apex of Jesus' earthly ministry. It was, well, a mountaintop experience—a high mark in the life of Jesus. One might be tempted to think he was simply homesick and wanted to visit his old friends—Moses and Elijah. The fact of the matter is, this mountaintop experience was not for his benefit but for a few sleepy disciples. Jesus is allowing them a glimpse through the veil so they can see his true glory. Peter's offer to build three shelters shows how far they have to go before they see Jesus for who he really is. He is not a colleague of the great prophets but their Master.

This is a colossal lesson. However, it is only half the lesson on this high hill. The most difficult vision is not God in the flesh but that self-same God suffering for our sins. We must never lose sight of Jesus' deity. Yet neither can we afford to forget his destiny. After all, the transfiguration is sandwiched between two bold predictions of his impending death. The transfiguration is the story of Jesus' life—God came to earth to die for our sins.

Pondering the Power of Jesus

- What is the most important event you ever slept through?
- What other events in Jesus' life are mirrored or shadowed in the transfiguration?
- What would be your response to a person who

claims that Jesus is just a moral teacher like many other religious leaders? What do you think Moses and Elijah would say to that person?

Meaning of the Text

To truly understand the transfiguration, we must back up six days. Six days ago was Peter's great confession. As you recall, Peter proclaimed Jesus as the Christ. Jesus praised Peter but then duly noted that this Christ must soon suffer in Jerusalem. That was such a foreign concept to Peter that he actually took Jesus off to the side and rebuked him. "How can the conquering king submit to a cross?" he thought. Jesus wheeled around to the Apostles and publicly rebuked his well-meaning nemesis. All that to say, with Jesus' first great self-revelation came the critical clarification that this Messiah would suffer.

This second great revelation of Jesus does the same thing. We don't just have a grand vision of God. We have a God enveloped in death. This transfiguration (Matt. 17:1-8) is surrounded by talk about Jesus' suffering (Matt. 16:21-23 & Matt. 17:9-13). When answering the question, "Who is Jesus?" to simply say, "God" is insufficient. We must tell the whole story of this God who robed himself in human flesh to die for a world gone bad. The broad brush strokes of this story remind us of that. Interestingly, so do the microscopic details. This text is full of rich and deep symbolism that tell the gospel in a nutshell. Look closely and you'll be amazed at what you see.

A voice from heaven validated Jesus. This takes us back to the baptism where God also said, "This is my beloved son." We remember too that this immersion was prophetic of death and resurrection. It too had something to do with remission of sins. Furthermore, when God declares Jesus to be his son, he is quoting himself at Psalm 2. What an incredible piece. Put down this book and take a minute to read that poem. There you will find a detailed description of Jesus' rejection by civil authorities who wanted to shed the shackles of God (cf. Acts 4:25-28). Yahweh scoffed, then huffed, then crushed. He crowned his honored son and put in his hand an iron scepter. Now he must be reckoned with as the ruler of the universe.

The three sleepy disciples give the aroma of Gethsemane. Both times they fall asleep at a critical moment. Both times they were on a mountain alone with the master. Both times death is in the air. The difference is in the lighting. Gethsemane was so dark, but there's enough light from the transfiguration to illuminate that garden grove. As we place the two peaks side by side we see in both a suffering God. Jesus wasn't trapped in the garden, he was destined for it.

The talk of "exodus" points toward Calvary. After all, when one thinks of the original exodus it comes with the trappings of a Passover lamb, liberation from bondage, and the crossing of a sea. These are the very images used to portray the Christian's pilgrimage to Jesus (cf. 1 Cor 10:1-4).

The white raiment and two witnesses remind us of the resurrection. There, too, we have two men (angels) dressed in white giving witness to Jesus. We also see Jesus' countenance was transformed. There is simply something about this scene that creates an expectation, a hope that transcends the gloomy talk of "exodus."

Somehow **the mountain itself** foreshadows the ascension. It feels like the mountain is as high as the Apostles can go, yet it's still far too shallow for the glory of Jesus. He simply must rise to the heavens, for even the heights of this earth can't contain his majesty.

There's even imagery of the second coming in the likes of **Moses and Elijah**. The latter, of course, never died. He was whisked away to heaven in a fiery chariot (2 Kgs. 2:11), which was why Jewish literature and lore so expected his return (Mal. 4:5-6). Moses did die but was buried by the very hand of God (Deut. 34:1,6). This led to rampant speculation about his return as well. In fact, between the writing of Malachi and Matthew, a Jewish book was penned entitled *The Assumption of Moses*, which predicted his bodily return to earth. Moses' own prophecy about a coming prophet like himself (cf. Deut. 18:15-18) gave hope to generations of Jews that a liberator would someday come. So here we have the quintessential national leader in Moses and the quintessential prophet in Elijah, both of whom were prophesied to return. So how does this look forward to Jesus' second coming? Well, the image is picked up again in Revelation 11:3-6 by two harbingers of Jesus' return.

I suppose that any one of these images could be brushed aside as coincidence. Taken together, however, they paint a striking picture of the purpose and power of the Lord. Encapsulated in this scene are the major events of Jesus' life: Baptism, Suffering, Death, Resurrection, Ascension, and Return. In short, Jesus is God in the flesh who redeems a fallen world through victorious suffering.

This grand portrait is huge, certainly too much for three weary disciples wiping sleep from their eyes. For them, the excitement is about Moses and Elijah. Well, one can certainly understand. For a Jewish boy, that would be big stuff. Two of the greatest leaders of Israelite history right there with them! They ought to be revered; they ought to be memorialized. Peter suggests they do just that. "Let's build booths and prolong this magnificent moment. Let's somehow recognize the immense blessing God has bestowed on us. Let's set side by side these three renowned leaders."

That was a problem, not because he wanted to respect the national leaders, but because he reduced Jesus to their equal. The one who recognized Jesus as the Christ less than one week ago now fails to fully see his significance on this mountain. He is like Moses, yes, but bigger. He is like Elijah, to be sure, but far greater. These two are types of Christ, but not his peers. Peter is about to learn that lesson in a big way.

A week ago when Peter attempted to discipline Jesus for his "cross talk" he found himself sorely rebuffed by the Son of God. This time, his silly suggestion is going to get him spanked by Yahweh himself who says, "This is my Son, listen to him." The lesson is still there for us to learn. Jesus is not a great moral teacher. He's not one among a few great leaders or religious giants. He stands, even on the highest mountain, without equal. He is not to be revered as a prophet, but feared as God.

Participating in the Power of Jesus

First, as a group or as an individual use a dictionary to define these words: awesome, majestic, and holy. With a clear understanding of those words, determine how they should affect your relationship with Jesus on a daily basis.

Secondly, determine how these words will affect eternity. What does an ideal day in the presence of Jesus look like for you? How do you see yourself interacting with him in heaven?

Thirdly, begin using these words in prayer when you address Jesus.

The world is poor because her fortune is buried in the sky and all her treasure maps are of the earth.

—Calvin Miller

The glory of God is man fully alive.

—Irenaeus

10 THE MIRROR OF THE BLIND MAN 10

Text: John 9:1-41 **Memory:** John 9:3-5

What's in a Name?

I have two older brothers. One is five years my elder and the other eight. My parents decided at birth to give each of us a name that began with the letter "J." Among the four of us, my sister included, there has never been an issue of mistaken identity. We are all unique, whether in appearance or personality. But for others, the distinction has not always been easy to make. Especially for the senior minister in our home church.

Each Sunday after the service wrapped up, he stood at the door greeting everyone. As a kid, I never could figure out how a guy could look so tall on stage and be so short in real life. I thought shaking his hand would give me an opportunity to check out his shoes and see if there were hidden stilts on them. But inevitably, when our family made it to the door and we were greeted, there was never time to check out his shoes, because we spent our time reminding him of our names.

He would rub my head and say, "Wow, hasn't Joe grown this week!" or "Isn't Jud turning out to be a fine young man!" The truth is, I hadn't grown an inch and I was quite the troublemaker so neither statements were true, and on top of that, my name was and still is Jon, not Joe or Jud. You see, he couldn't keep the three of us straight.

Well, one Sunday during the service, our preacher finished his sermon, had the congregation stand up, and then began to scan the crowd for someone to close the service in prayer. He looked toward our family and said, "I am going to ask Jon Weece to close us out in prayer this morning." It was like the words came out of his mouth in slow motion! I was only seven years old at the time. At that age, I was still taking naps during the service or coloring on the back of the bulletin. As color left my face, my jaw dropped and my brothers pointed at me and laughed. Heads in the church actually bowed, the room went quiet, and I nearly lost my breakfast! In the awkwardness of the moment, my mom pinched my oldest brother's arm, knowing that our preacher had again confused us and really wanted him to pray. So, in a moment of true valor, a moment deserving of a purple heart in my seven-year-old mind, my brother prayed in my place.

And sure enough, at the end of the service as our family filed out of the sanctuary, our preacher again shook our hands and said to my brother Joe, "Thank you, Jon, for praying this morning."

In the following chapter, Jesus is once again called to defend his claim to deity. Was he who he said he was? Could he really be God? Read on and you, like the blind man in this story, may see there isn't much of a case for mistaken identity.

Overview of the Text

Of the thousands of miracles John could have recorded in his book, he only chose seven. Why? Because he's not trying to impress us with the quantity of Jesus' miraculous works, but transform us through their quality (cf. John 20:30-31). Through seven miraculous signs he holds up a mirror and lets us see our own pilgrimage to Christ. With each, he magnifies a particular aspect of our journey and how to successfully experience the deepest life in Jesus. He uses the blind man to shed light on a particularly important issue: Is Jesus still worth following at the expense of all else? The Pharisees pounced on the blind man for being healed on the Sabbath day and demanded that he denounce Jesus. At the cost of his family, friends, and faith, he stood firm with the one who helped him see. So there it is, the question of the day: Now that you see, can you ever be forced to turn a blind eye to him whom you know to be Truth?

Pondering the Power of Jesus

- ☧ Are you as verbal about the healing Jesus has provided in your life as the blind man in this story? What intimidates you most about sharing what Jesus has done for you with others?
- ☧ Why do you think Jesus used spit and mud to heal a man?
- ☧ Do you know anyone who has been seriously sick or physically crippled who was told this indicated sin in their life?

Meaning of the Text

He was a beggar because he was born blind. He was one of the thousands of "throwaway" people who, through no fault of his own, was a drain on society rather than a participant. Remember, this is before the days of disability acts and handicap accessories. His only contribution, really, is to enable pious Jews to feel good about themselves as they rattle his tin cup with coins on their way into the temple.

As the disciples pass by, they ask Jesus whether the man himself was to blame for his predicament or whether this was punishment for what his parents had done. Neither option seems palatable to us, yet they were common fare for the day. Jesus, seemingly disinterested in assigning blame, looks to the solution. Instead of asking, "Whose fault is this?" he asks, "What can be done about this?" or, more accurately, "How can God be glorified through this?" With that, he spit on the ground, slapped some mud in the man's eyes and sent him to Siloam to wash. This particular pool is a half mile to a mile from the temple (depending on what gate he sat by) and down a very steep embankment. This poor fellow will be awhile. While we're waiting for him to return, we might want to pause and take notice of what has just happened. The name of the pool is "Siloam." That is a Hebrew word that means "sent." Thus the blind man was sent to "sent" to wash to see. That is thick with symbolism and mirrors our own story. We too were blind but washed in order to see and so we were sent to send others to Jesus.

When he gains his sight, he has good news to tell. Who, pray tell, are the most logical recipients of this most wondrous news? Why his neighbors, of course. For the first time in his life he sees them. Oddly, they are the ones who don't recognize *him*. They debate about his identity. In defense of himself (literally), he tells them what happened. In the natural course of his testimony he mentions Jesus. Suddenly bells and whistles blew and red flags were raised. "Wait a minute," they said, "That's the Galilean troublemaker the Sanhedrin is after!" Their sympathy for the guy is underwhelming. They are more concerned about not getting mixed up in this troubling affair than they are in rejoicing with their friend. So they turn him over to the authorities. This will make for a roller-coaster of a day for the blind man.

Suddenly his self-defense takes a different turn. Remember, this guy has been a professional beggar all his life and now he stands before the powerful elite leaders of the nation. I love this guy; he doesn't even flinch. When asked how he was healed, he gives a brief rendition of the events: "He put mud in my eyes. I washed, and now I see." Of course, since this transpired on the Sabbath day, there will be problems—not only for the blind man but for the Sanhedrin itself. You see, they were divided over the miracle. Some argued adamantly that God's prophet would keep the Sabbath. "On the other hand," some said, "if he's such a nefarious sinner then how can he perform such wondrous signs?"

When they can't come to any consensus they turn to the blind man and ask, "What do you have to say about the man?" Let me assure you, they aren't wanting his opinion *per se*. They are assessing the amount of damage control that will be necessary. After all, an ex-blind beggar is going to get a lot of notable press. If he's enamored with Jesus, they do, indeed, have problems. His answer confirmed their worst fears: "He's a prophet."

Their preliminary investigation didn't go so well. Not only does the blind man confess Jesus, but many of the Pharisees start to lean in that direction as well. Trying an alternate tactic, they call in the man's parents. "Is this really your son who was supposedly born blind?" they ask. Obviously, they are trying to deny any miracle took place in the first place. That would be the easiest way out. No good—they confirm with certainty both that he is their son and that he was born blind. The couple does, however, deny any knowledge about his present well-being. Now that was almost certainly a bold-faced lie. You mean to tell me the young man goes and preaches to the neighborhood but doesn't tell Mom and Dad how he was healed? There's no way! This couple is not ignorant of their son's condition, they are scared of the Sanhedrin. They take seriously the threat of excommunication. It was, indeed, a merciless condition that drove one out of all significant social and economic contacts.

 That's strike two and their options are thin, so they summon the man back in for a second round of questioning. They now realize they can't deny an impressive miracle took place. Their only recourse is to somehow distance Jesus from the miracle. They demand the blind man "give glory to God." That is an idiomatic way of saying, "Give glory *exclusively* to God." It is also asking him to admit (even repent) of his previous error of attributing to Jesus the power of God. This guy is too sharp for that. He may have been blind, but he's never been deaf. He sits quietly just outside the temple gate, listening to the debates inside and meditating on the truth. In a towering, cynical statement he says, "I don't know if Jesus is a sinner as you say. I do know this: I was blind and now I see."

There's really nowhere else to go in this investigation so they start back at the beginning: "How did he heal you?" Not wanting to get on that merry-go-round again he asked, "Do you also want to become his disciples?" Now that nearly sent them into apoplexy. Why on earth is this guy so belligerent when he's got so much to lose? He could get kicked out of the synagogue! Hello . . . He's blind, he's never been included in these social circles anyway. Unlike the lame man of John 5 who gave Jesus up for fear of the Pharisees, this guy has already thought through the implications. Why join a club that refuses to give glory to God for an obvious miracle?

They begin to pummel the blind man with insults: "You low-life sinner. We know God spoke to Moses, but we don't know where this guy came from." You can assault this guy all you want but he's not one to be intimidated. He rifles back, "That's amazing that you don't know where Jesus is from. After all, as religious leaders I'd think you'd put a premium on getting to know a man whose miracles obviously identify him as God's man." Uh oh, that probably crossed the line. He's out on his ear.

When Jesus found out, he looked him up and asked, "Do

you believe in the Messiah?" The blind man sees Jesus for the first time but recognizes him by the sound of his voice. "Tell me who he is," the man said, "And I'll believe in him." Jesus replied, "I am he." Notice how the man's confession has grown. In verse 11 he identified Jesus as "the man they call Jesus." By verse 17 he becomes "a prophet." In verse 33 he acknowledges that he's "come from God." And by verse 38 he proclaims him Lord.

Likewise, we, too, grow in our perception of Jesus. In fact, the closer we are to losing friends, family, and religion, the more certain we must be about his identity. Conversely, the clearer our view of Jesus becomes, the more willing we are to sacrifice for him. For when he gives us sight to see him clearly, we know with certainty he's worth all we sacrifice.

Participating in the Power of Jesus

One of the ways to see Jesus clearly is to put yourself around brothers and sisters in Christ who have made those sacrifices. It's rare to find them in this country but you will find them overseas. Decide to step out of your comfort zone by joining a short-term missions trip to a country where you will gain a fresh perspective on sacrifice and the person of Jesus. You will be amazed by the difference one trip can make in the development of your faith. For information on short-term opportunities, check with these mission organizations: Team Expansion, Food for the Hungry, Fellowship of Associates of Medical Evangelism (FAME), and Christ In Youth (CIY).

11 11

THE POWER OF JESUS OVER DEATH

11 11

If you attempt to talk with a dying man about sports or business, he is no longer interested. He now sees other things as more important. People who are dying recognize what we often forget, that we are standing on the brink of another world.

—William Law

I think of death as a glad awakening from this troubled sleep which we call life; as an emancipation from a world which, beautiful though it may be, is still a land of captivity.

—Lyman Abbott

Text: John 11:1-44 **Memory:** John 11:25-26

Resuscitation or Resurrection?

Twenty-seven people are banking on the idea that modern science will someday find or engineer a fountain of youth. Those twenty-seven people, all deceased, are "patients" of the Alcor Life Extension Institute in Scottsdale, Arizona, where their bodies have been frozen in liquid nitrogen at minus 320 degrees Fahrenheit awaiting the day when medical science discovers a way to make death and aging a thing of the past.

Ten of the patients paid $120,000 to have their entire body frozen. Seventeen of the patients paid $50,000 to have only their head frozen, hoping that molecular technology will one day be able to grow a whole new body from their head or its cells. It sounds like science fiction, but it's called cryonics.

As you can imagine, cryonics has its share of critics and skeptics. Of course, Stephen Bridge, president of Alcor, cautions, "We have to tell people that we don't even really know if it will work yet."

Nevertheless, Thomas Donaldson, a fifty-year-old member of Alcor who hasn't yet taken advantage of its services, brushed aside the naysayers and explained to a reporter why he's willing to give cryonics a try: "For some strange reason, I like being alive. . . . I don't want to die."

There is a better investment on life. For those who are friends and not enemies of Jesus, death brings about that certainty of resurrection that cryonics will never provide. Just ask Lazarus.

Overview of the Text

We come to the seventh sign in John and the greatest of all Jesus' miracles. The previous signs have unveiled the incomparable Christ who turns water to wine, heals from a distance, feeds 5,000, walks on water, and gives sight to blind eyes. These pale compared to our Lord's victory over death—the fiercest enemy of humanity. Indeed, Jesus has already raised two others from the dead: the widow's son at Nain (Luke 7:11-17) and Jairus's daughter (Matt. 9:23-26; Mark 5:37-43; Luke 8:51-56). But when he raises Larazus, he takes resuscitation to a whole new level. The other two were raised soon after their departure. In the case of Lazarus, it was after an interval of four days. That is more significant in its Palestinian setting than it is to us, for the Jews believed the disembodied spirit hovered about the corpse for three days after death. Thus Jesus isn't merely performing spectacular CPR; he really does control the forces of the afterlife.

Pondering the Power of Jesus

- What scares you the most about dying?
- Have you ever been to a funeral service where there was no hope? Describe that funeral.
- What false sense of hope does our world have about death and the life to come?

The Power of Jesus over Death

⁂ Why do you think people are so uneasy about death?

Meaning of the Text

Jesus is a full two days away from Bethany when the servants bring him the bad news of Lazarus' precarious situation. Little do they know that at that very time, Lazarus' life is ebbing away. They are ignorantly cheered however with Jesus' promise, "This will not end in death. Instead, God will be glorified through this." Off they go, back to Bethany, undoubtedly pleased at the good news.

When they arrive with the happy announcement, they are informed that Lazarus has been dead for two days. Confusion sets in. They can't really blame Jesus for not healing Lazarus. After all, he wasn't given enough time. But why did he say that it would not end in death when it obviously did! Martha, our budding young theologian, attributes it to allegorical speech. That is, *ultimately*, on the day of judgment, Lazarus will live. While that is true, it is *not* what Jesus meant.

Meanwhile, Jesus announces to the boys that it is time to return to Judea to heal Lazarus. Had you been there you would have protested too! That's suicidal! The Sanhedrin has put out wanted posters on every telephone pole in Palestine. They want Jesus dead and he plans on walking right through their home turf. The boys aren't so warm to this idea. It was Thomas, the so-called doubter, that said, "All right, then, let's go to Judea and die with him." In a sense, this is prophetic. Thomas knows that in giving Lazarus life, Jesus himself will forfeit his. While that didn't literally happen on this occasion, if you use this as a lens and look through your telescope just two months out, you'll see clearly the story of Jesus.

By the time they arrive, Lazarus has been entombed for four days. Martha was the first to hear of Jesus' arrival. She races to him with the choral refrain that had permeated their home for the last four days, "If only you had been here, my brother would not have died." This statement sparks one of the most incredible theological discourses in all the Bible. Jesus promises Martha that Lazarus will rise. She accepts his words as true, but casts them deep into the future. The paradox is that she is very right yet completely wrong, as is so often the case with those of us who pursue the promises of God. We accept the words as true, seeing only half the majesty. We look forward to what we'll obtain in heaven while being blind to the present reality of the glories of Christ.

The apex of this theological discourse is Jesus' magisterial statement of verse 25: "I am the resurrection and the life. He who believes in me will live even though he dies." This is the fifth of the "I Am" statements in John. She replies, "I believe that you are the Christ, the Son of God, who was to come into the world." Her confession is noble. It rivals any other in the entire book (cf. 1:29,41,45,49; 4:42; 6:68-69; 11:27). Martha believes Jesus gives life, just not literally—at least not yet.

When Martha returns home, she tells Mary about Jesus' arrival. Mary, of course, makes a beeline to her Master. Curiously, she comes to Jesus with the exact same opening line that Martha does, "Lord, if only you had been here, Lazarus would not have died." On the lips of Martha these words sparked a theological debate. From Mary, however, they elicited an entirely different response. Jesus became highly emotional. The first word used to describe how he felt is *embrimaomai* (cf. Matt. 9:30; Mark 1:43; 14:5). It has a flavor of frustration, even anger. The second word is *tarassō,* which is used to describe angry waves on an ocean (Isa. 24:14, LXX). Jesus is really bothered. Here's something I find fascinating. While Martha's words elicit theology, Mary's elicit emotion. There was something in her faith that cut the discussion to the quick. It got to the heart of the issue. Don't get me wrong, Jesus' little theological dissertation is essential. We need such words. But all too often we talk all too much and never get to the real issue—people are suffering under the heavy cost of sin. We live under the oppression of the curse and only Jesus can liberate us from our ultimate enemy of death. We can talk all we want, but until we weep we will not approach a solution to the problem.

Why is Jesus so bothered? Why does he stand before the tomb and weep (v. 35) even though he knows he'll raise Lazarus in a moment? Surely it has something to do with his frustration with death. He hates this unnatural state of affairs. He deplores the pain and suffering of the human predicament incurred by the curse. He is saddened by our lack of faith. Not only do so many reject him, but even his followers seem incapable of seeing all the richness he has in store for them. Standing at the grave, the front lines of battle with his nemesis, he is reminded of how far we've fallen and how far he has to go to restore us to the Father. He's not weeping for Lazarus; that will be corrected in a moment. He's weeping for a world gone so desperately awry.

Against Martha's protest, Jesus commands the stone at the entrance to be moved out of the way. He gives the word, a shout that pierces the underworld. The crowd's consternation gives way to awe as the shrouded figure emerges up the steps. Wrapped from head to toe he wiggles his way out the entrance. Jesus orders his head to be unwrapped and one wonders what Lazarus had to say. I suspect he was the only one who spoke . . . at least at first.

Why mention the fact that his head was unwrapped? Was this necessary so Lazarus wouldn't suffocate? Was it so he could give testimony to God's power or reveal the wonders of the netherworld? Interestingly, the word for "cloth" (v. 44) refers specifically to the head covering and is used only one other time in the book of John (20:7). There it refers to the cloth that was used to cover Jesus' head in the tomb. That was what John saw that caused him to believe that the Lord had indeed been raised. Undoubtedly, the cloth is a sign in both texts that binds them together. When this shroud is removed we see clearly what is really going on here. Lazarus' story is really our own and is only made possible when Jesus takes upon himself our suffering. It is through the resurrection of Christ that we too have such secure hope to be raised up with him.

Participating in the Power of Jesus

Take the time to plan out your funeral. Whom would you have speak? Sing? What would you want said of you when you die? Will your faith in Jesus be a surprise to those who attend the funeral? Who needs to be there to hear about the hope you have?

May 25

12 12

JESUS' LAST TWO "CONVERTS"

12 12

> It seems that more than ever the compulsion today is to identify, to reduce someone to what is on the label. To identify is to control, to limit. To love is to call by name, and so open the wide gates of creativity.
>
> —*Madeleine L'Engle*
>
> It is easy to be brave from a safe distance.
>
> —*Aesop*

Text: Luke 18:35–19:10 **Memory:** Luke 19:9-10

Transformation

Life in east Harlem, New York is worlds away from what most of us experience on a daily basis. For a 12-year-old, half-Italian boy named Billy the streets provided a daily lesson in survival. His dad ran out when Billy was one year old, also leaving behind a wife and two daughters. Billy's young life resembled a war. Daily battles were fought with fists, knives, and guns. He had been tapped by local gang members to be a drug runner. Big time gang leaders used boys his age as errand boys, knowing they probably wouldn't encounter the same fate as older boys who didn't meet expectations. The men he worked for were known killers and on several occasions held Billy at gunpoint, threatening to kill him for mistakes his bosses were making. The drama was real, the stakes were high.

As part of his initiation, Billy was forced into a room

where a prostitute was waiting for him. At the age of 12, Billy's life took a turn for the worse. Drug and alcohol abuse would be commonplace.

As a teenager, Billy excelled in the game of basketball. Local playgrounds served as stages on which he performed, and it didn't take long for Billy to gain the reputation of a legend. Basketball made him a god, and many in his community lived vicariously through him, knowing that it might just be his ticket out of the projects. He earned the nicknames "Billy NBA," and "White Jesus" and was regarded by many as a possible NBA draft pick in the future. The *New York Daily News* did a feature article on him. You see, Billy was one of four white kids who attended a high school with 2,500 African-American students. At his first home basketball game, fans laughed at this white kid who walked out on the court. Following the opening tip-off, Billy took the ball, dribbled the length of the court, and dunked over the opposing team's tallest player. That dunk is still talked about on street corners and in barber shops. The game literally came to a stop as the crowd ran onto the floor and danced for over 20 minutes!

Following his high school feats, Billy was paid to play college ball at a university in Louisiana. His life continued toward destruction. He was living in the fast lane of alcohol, women, and fame when an injury changed the course of his basketball career. He transferred to a small college in Kentucky, of all places, and met Carolynn, a strong Christian from an eastern section of Kentucky that Billy says, "Rivals the east side of Harlem!" Billy and Carolynn married 18 years ago. And in the time since, Billy has hit rock bottom on several occasions, forcing him each time to evaluate where he was headed in life. The immoral lifestyle, the anger and rage from his childhood, and the potential threat of liver failure and AIDS were finally dealt with. The hole in Billy's life was filled with an insatiable appetite for the things of God. His wife's prayers were answered. She didn't give up on him, because God hadn't given up on Billy yet. And last Christmas, his 16-year-old daughter said to him, "Dad, I used to be afraid of you, but God has changed you and I'm no longer afraid."

Today, Billy is a man I look up to. His laugh, his love for the lost, his prayer life, his heart for worship, are all contagious. He is a new creation in Christ. He is your brother. And now, he truly is a "White Jesus" to everyone he comes in contact with.

Overview of the Text

At the tail end of Jesus' ministry he encounters two men: Bartimaeus and Zacchaeus. The first is a blind beggar, the second is a political power broker. Both seek Jesus; both have their eyes opened and their lives transformed. One is an up-and-outer, the other a down-and-outer. Yet both fit into Jesus' plan to seek and save the lost. It is as if they stand as book ends on either side of humanity, inviting all who stand in the middle to follow their lead in chasing after Jesus.

Pondering the Power of Jesus

- Do you know a modern day Bartimaeus? Zacchaeus? If so, describe them to your group.
- When was the last time you met someone as hungry to meet and know Jesus as Bartimaeus and Zacchaeus?
- Have you ever been guilty of keeping someone from meeting Jesus?
- Was there ever a time that you cried out to Jesus as Bartimaeus did?

Meaning of the Text

Jericho sits about 14 miles east of Jerusalem. It is an oasis in the desert. It is strewn with palms and figs, mineral springs and deep traditions. Because of its natural resources, it had become a center for commerce. The trade routes from Egypt and Syria,

Arabia and Babylon all crisscrossed here. Her population was ethnically and economically diverse. On a normal day the streets teemed with people from all over the Mediterranean: Jews and Arabs, Syrians and Egyptians, Greeks and Mesopotamians, and, of course, the ever-present Roman forces. On this particular day, however, the crowds swelled. You see, it was one week before Passover and the roads were jammed with pilgrims making the final leg of their trek to the Holy City. On top of that, Jesus came to town with his own considerable company of followers. The scene was electric. There were wall-to-wall bodies all crooking their necks to get a glimpse of this miracle-working sage. They'll not be disappointed.

On the outskirts of town sat a blind man named Bartimaeus. He was a beggar. With no Disabilities Act and no social services, that was about his only option. When he hears the crowd and learns that Jesus is behind it, he makes a scene. "Have mercy on me, Son of David," he shouts. Those nearest try to shut him up. After all, when a dignitary such as Jesus comes to town, you want to put your best foot forward. You want to hide these sorts of indigents. But this particular indigent gets indignant and shouts all the louder. He stops Jesus in his tracks. The Master calls for him. Bartimaeus is quickly escorted to the center of the parade by the very ones who had just shushed him. "What do you want?" Jesus asks (as if he didn't know). "I want to see!" he replied. The next thing he knows, light floods his eyes. If you think he was loud before, you should hear him now. Laughter, praise, song, and dance erupt spontaneously and spread throughout the crowded streets of Jericho.

As mass jubilation made its way through the city, the people pushed and shoved to get even a glimpse of the Master. One of Jericho's citizens tried in vain, but he was too small to elbow his way to the front of the line. Don't get me wrong, he was quite a powerful guy, but only in the IRS office, not on the streets. Zacchaeus was the highest local official in the tax collection machine of the Roman regime. He was, indeed, Jewish but was working for the "enemy." Because of that he was ostracized and hated as the Benedict Arnold of his own community.

Why he wants to see Jesus we can only guess. By his response we can assume it was more than mere curiosity. Since he can't get to Jesus directly, he runs up the street ahead of the parade and climbs a sycamore-fig tree. It was a great tree for climbing with low, thick branches, and it's large, lush leaves might hide him as he goes out on a limb to see Jesus. It's quite a sight to see this little guy up in a tree wearing a pinstriped toga; climbing trees was way beneath his dignity.

His efforts are not in vain. Jesus passes by and stops. He turns his head up and over, looks straight at our little friend and says, "Zacchaeus, come down immediately. I simply must stay at your house today." The crowds go wild. "What?! You're going to *his* house? But Lord, don't you know who he is?" Apparently Jesus knew precisely who he was. After all, he called him by name! Those who pressed hardest and wrestled their way into Jesus' inner circle began to protest. "Lord, come to our house instead. We deserve you. This man is a sinner. Come hold our babies, come bless our homes. We deserve your teaching and touch, not this scalawag." But you know how difficult it is to change Jesus' mind once he's got it set. Everyone in the crowd was put out with Jesus, probably even his own disciples . . . except for one. Matthew surely choked back tears as he reminisced about his own transformation. He knew what was about to take place.

Zacchaeus stands up with a striking announcement: "I'm going to right here and now give half of my possessions to the poor. Moreover, I'll repay anyone I've wronged fourfold." Consider for a moment just how substantial this offer is. He is the equivalent of a multimillionaire who's built his empire through questionable taxation that bordered on extortion. If he carries through with this, his fortunes will be reduced to something like 10% of his former assets. His life will change radically. Talk about a living parable of the pearl of great price. He found Jesus just in the nick of time and it cost him everything.

There are two striking things about Bartimaeus and Zacchaeus. First, this event is late in the life of Jesus. In fact, as near as we can tell, they met Jesus one week to the day before he was killed. One can only imagine the wrenching pain they went through watching their newfound friend die such a despicable death. They almost missed him. Had Bartimaeus shouted one less time or a few decibels lower, he would have died destitute on the streets of Jericho. Had Zacchaeus given up when the crowds shoved him aside, had he decided to listen from the back rather than embarrassing himself by climbing a tree, he could have remained in his opulent squalor. They came so close to missing it all. The lesson is clear. When Jesus passes by, you grab hold of him and hang on for dear life. One can never tell what another week will bring.

The second thing that strikes us about Bartimaeus and Zacchaeus is how very different they were. One is a blind beggar, the other a governmental power broker. Yet both craved Jesus. Bartimaeus was a down-and-outer, Zacchaeus an up-and-outer, yet both needed the Lord. Jesus called both to his side. To one he gave sight, to the other he gave sonship by declaring him, too, a child of Abraham (Luke 19:9). Both were blind but now could see.

Thus the story ends with the purpose statement of Jesus' life: "The Son of Man came to seek and to save that which was lost" (Luke 19:10). From the rich to the poor, Jesus seeks to save the lost. From the famous to infamous, from sinner to saint, from Jew to Gentile, male and female, intellect and commoner, Jesus recklessly pursues salvation for his beloved. Surely you stand somewhere in the middle between these two. Surely you stand in the center of Luke 19:10, right in the heart of God's grand plan. Don't wait for seven days to respond.

Participating in the Power of Jesus

Find and read the children's classic, *The Giving Tree* by Shel Silverstein.

June 1

> A reform is a correction of abuses; a revolution is a transfer of power.
> —E. G. Bulwer-Lytton
>
> The wishbone will never replace the backbone.
> —William Henry
>
> Behold the turtle. He makes progress only when he sticks his neck out.
> —James B. Conant

13 13

CLEANSING THE TEMPLE

13 13

Text: Mark 11:15-18 **Memory:** Mark 11:17-18

Victory! At the 1994 Winter Olympics, held in Hamar, Norway, the name Dan took on a very special meaning.

At his first Olympics in 1984 as an eighteen-year-old, Dan Jansen finished fourth in the 500-meter race, beaten for a bronze medal by only sixteen hundredths of a second. At his second Olympics in Calgary in 1988, on the morning he was to skate the 500 meters, he received a phone call from America. His twenty-seven-year-old sister, Jane, who had been fighting leukemia for over a year, was dying. Dan spoke to her over the phone, but she was too sick to say anything in return. Their brother Mike relayed Jane's message: She wanted Dan to race for her. Before Dan skated that afternoon, however, he received the news that Jane had died. When he took to the ice, perhaps he tried too hard for his sister. In the

500 meters, he slipped and fell in the first turn. He had never fallen before in a race. Four days later in the 1,000-meter race, he fell again, this time, in a straightaway.

At his third Olympics in 1992, he was expected to win the 500 meters, where he had been regarded as the best sprinter in the world. But again he struggled and finished in fourth place. At his fourth Olympics, he announced that he would retire after his 1000-meter race. Midway through the race, Dan was on pace to break a world record. With 200 meters left in the race everyone's heart skipped a beat. Dan didn't fall, but he slipped, touching his hand to the ice. He was able to regain control, kept skating, and finished the race. When he looked at the scoreboard and saw "New World Record," beside his name, his hands went to his head in amazement and relief. He had finally won a gold medal. He looked heavenward, acknowledging his late sister Jane. He was asked to skate a victory lap following the awards ceremony. The lights were turned out, and a single spotlight illuminated Dan's last lap around the Olympic track, with a gold medal around his neck, roses in one arm, and his baby daughter—named Jane—in his other arm.

The gold medal had eluded him for a decade. In his previous seven races, he had been unable to secure a gold medal. Alongside a snow-covered road outside of Hamar, the sight of his first Olympics, someone put a hand-lettered sign which simply read, "Dan." It spoke volumes about what the world thought of a man whose futile Olympic efforts had finally ended in triumph.

Sometimes a name, a name alone, says it all. We've been aiming the spotlight at one man through these books, but the real triumph of Jesus is just beginning.

Overview of the Text

When Jesus cleansed the temple he was making an obvious statement about the status of Jewish religion in his day. It clearly needed renovation. But his actions also had significant political ramifications. This cleansing was not merely a call to reform religion but the entire political system. The Sadducees who controlled the temple were engorged with wealth from peasant worshipers. The King of the Jews was an Edomite named Herod who was a collaborator with Rome. Their peacekeeping forces swarmed the streets of God's holy city, importing pagan religion and practices. It was time for radical reform. Jesus' actions demand just that.

Pondering the Power of Jesus

- What are your first impressions after reading Mark 11:15-18?
- What kind of political stakes were involved when Jesus cleansed the temple?
- When Jesus cleansed the temple, he was seeking a reform. Describe the kind of temple Jesus is really after.

Meaning of the Text

It is now Monday morning of Christ's final week. It's going to be a huge day. To see just how large it is, however, we need to place it against the backdrop of the previous day's events. Jesus marched into the temple to have a look around. He came from the east, over the Mount of Olives. Rather than walking, he rode a young donkey. Typically, this was a sign of a royal inauguration. The myriad who followed Jesus didn't miss the Messianic import of this highly symbolic action. They cut palm branches along the way and laid them down to create the cultural equivalent of a red carpet. They even took off their cloaks and laid them on the ground for the donkey to walk on. Literally, Jesus got the *royal* treatment.

From the temple mount below, the High Priest and his officials could hardly have missed the clamoring entourage as they descended the slopes of Olivet and swarmed the temple mount. Nor would this have escaped the notice of the Roman garrison stationed at the Fortress of Antonia just northwest of the Temple. Given the fact that it was the Passover festival and hundreds of thousands of patriotic Jews converged upon Jerusalem, the Roman military was on peak alert for an uprising. This is precisely the kind of thing they feared the most. The soldiers had their hands on their swords; the Sadducees were on pins and needles. Jesus just came in, took a look around, and then retreated back to Bethany for the night.

It was morning now and Jesus made a grand entrance. There in the temple courts were cages with birds, pens of sheep, ropes around the necks of bulls and goats. Off to the side were money changers, giving travelers kosher currency with which to purchase a sacrificial animal. The exchange rate was often as high as 15%; the price of "blessed" animals was outrageous. It was clearly a scam.

Jesus went ballistic. Tables flew, tempers flared, animals bolted, coins were scattered. It was pandemonium, but nothing they've not seen before. John says Jesus did this at the beginning of his ministry as well (John 2:12-25), only that time he actually wove the rope into a whip and waylaid the merchants. Jesus' public ministry both began and ended with an assault on the temple. How could he get away with it? I mean, he marched into the nerve center of the Jewish nation and single-handedly shut down business. How? Well, one thing we need to know is that this bazaar in the temple was quite unpopular with the people (Pharisees included). There were only a handful of aristocrats that benefited from the scandal. They had the power but they were badly outnumbered by all these pilgrims that simply adored Jesus. If they so much as bristled against the Galilean, they would have a bloodbath on their hands. All they can do is watch from the sidelines and seethe.

The tension is thick, the celebration rampant. But there is more at stake than a quiet place to pray. Jesus is not simply "cleaning house." This is quite a bold threat to the whole of the temple structure. What we have here is more than a religious impulse; this is a political statement. To see it clearly we must understand several things. First, the dominant view of the Messiah was not a preacher or even a prophet, but a king who reigned on God's behalf. Second, the temple was not merely equivalent to our church building. It was a financial institution where large sums of money were guarded, as well as a military fortress, fully armed for the event of war. In fact, in 70 A.D. when Jerusalem finally fell, the temple was the last stronghold of the city. Thus, whoever controlled the temple controlled the throne. Right now the power is shared by Pilate the governor, Herod the royal impostor, and the aristocratic Sadducean collaborators.

In Jesus' mind that just won't do. So he threatens the temple with a deliberate, yet veiled declaration. Specifically, he quotes two Old Testament prophets who also stood in these sacred precincts and threatened destruction barring repentance. The first was Isaiah (56:7), "My house will be called a house of prayer for all nations." Well, what a nice thing to say! That is even politically correct—opening up the Jewish temple to multicultural worship. However, if one goes back to the context of Isaiah's statement one will find that these words are hardly "nice." The entire chapter is a call to inclusion. Go ahead and read it. Not just the outer court was to be opened but the entire edifice, and not just to foreigners but even eunuchs. Clearly, Jesus isn't just altering the outskirts of the temple but calling for a transformation of the whole.

The second passage is even more poignant. It comes from Jeremiah (7:11), that weeping prophet. It says, "You've made it a den of robbers." Based on Isaiah, Jesus merely says, "Big changes are coming." Now he says, "If you don't make these changes, God will eradicate the whole building!" Again, read the context of Jeremiah 7:11. "Reform your ways and your actions, and I will let you live in this place" (v. 3) The implication is clear: If you don't reform your ways, I'll wipe you out. You know what? He did it in the days of Jeremiah. In 586 B.C. Nebuchadnezzar marched on the city and leveled it. Jesus said it was going to happen again. He was right. In 66–70 A.D. the Romans came and ravaged the city and burned the temple to the ground. Jesus is not making an idle threat here. The only options he leaves are total reformation or total destruction.

Several days later, during Jesus' trial, the first accusation made against him was that he threatened the temple. While they couldn't prove the charge, they were quite correct. His words were so carefully couched that he couldn't be pinned in a court of law. Yet his actions spoke louder than his words and unmistakably declared the demise of this temple.

What does all this mean today? For one thing, it means there is no Jewish temple. There is no place for animal sacrifice. The book of Hebrews has a little something to say about that. Since Jesus himself was the perfect sacrifice, the Old Testament offerings are now irrelevant. The physical temple is obsolete. Second, not only is Jesus our perfect sacrifice, he is, in fact, the temple itself. He promised this the first time he cleansed the temple in John 2:19, "Destroy this temple and in three days I'll raise it up again." He did transform the temple precincts into a place where all ethnic groups are welcome. That place is his own body, now embodied in the church he established. Finally, Jesus is the king he claimed to be. He's not just a religious teacher or an eschatological prophet. He is a ruler of a very real and global kingdom. He didn't come merely to save our souls but to institute a nation. We are engaged in a grand enterprise of the kingdom of God, which includes a great high priest, a final sacrifice, and a temple open to the entire world.

Read the book of Hebrews in the next week and highlight everything it says about the temple.

About the Authors

Mark Moore is Professor of New Testament at Ozark Christian College, teaching in the areas of Life of Christ, Acts, and Bible Interpretation. Mark did his undergraduate work at Ozark Christian College. He went on to earn a Masters in Education from Incarnate Word College in San Antonio, Texas, while pastoring a bilingual church there. Later he earned a Masters in Religious Studies from Southwest Missouri State University. He returned to Ozark to teach in the fall of 1990.

Mark is the author of a number of books, including other works on the Life of Christ: a two-volume set entitled *The Chronological Life of Christ,* and the more devotional *Encounters with Christ.* He is a popular speaker for both adult and youth conferences.

Mark makes his home in Joplin, Missouri, where his favorite place is with his wife, Barbara, and two teenage children, Josh and Megan, who both know and honor the Lord.

Jon Weece is currently ministering with Southland Christian Church in Lexington, Kentucky. He began in the summer of 2000 on the Teaching Team and as an Adult Discipleship Associate. Jon has served four years as a missionary in Haiti.

He graduated with a Bachelor of Biblical Literature degree from Ozark Christian College in Joplin, Missouri. He and his wife Allison live in Lexington. Jon is passionate about being a good husband and dad. He also enjoys a good Sunday afternoon drive, cooking steaks on the grill, reading a good book, and fishing for fish as well as for men.